A COLORNI-HIRSCHMAN INTERNATIONAL INSTITUTE 4

The Final Year: 1943–44
Genesis of a Perspective

Eugenio Colorni

The Final Year: 1943–44
Genesis of a Perspective

Edited by Luca Meldolesi
Translated from Italian by Michael Gilmartin

Bordighera Press

Library of Congress Control Number: 2020951993

Printed in the United States.

Published by
BORDIGHERA PRESS
John D. Calandra Italian American Institute
25 W. 43rd Street, 17th Floor
New York, NY 10036

A Colorni-Hirschman International Institute 4
ISBN 978–1–59954–179–2

TABLE OF CONTENTS

We should remember the gold medal given in his memory as a gold medal to the Roman Resistance; we should remember his every step, every move he made for Rome, because we are truly talking about a hero of the Roman Resistance. But it wasn't just our partisan comrade Angelo that we lost, we lost one who would have been, and already was, a true political guide; we lost a great and slightly older brother; we lost someone who, even though at a certain moment his more or less intense political commitment had to cease, would certainly have been a great beacon, a great moral inspiration, even for Italian political life up to the present day.

— Giuliano Vassalli

Speech at the Presentation of the Viareggio Presidente Award, given to *Eugenio Colorni. Ora e sempre,* by Leo Solari, July 1980 (Envelope 1, File 7, Solari fund).

INTRODUCTION

1. I have long believed that Eugenio Colorni's involvement as a protagonist in the Roman Resistance of 1943–1944 holds an important lesson that represents a key theoretical and practical element in the individual and collective mosaic that I have repeatedly sought to explore, at least since I met Albert Hirschman back in 1983.[1]

But up until a short time ago, the road I will be attempting to follow in the pages below appeared to be closed off.[2] This was because action precedes reflection,[3] and unfortunately Eugenio never had the chance to reflect on what he had witnessed. In addition, the testimony that has come down to us from his comrades in that struggle, while often copious, is inevitably unsystematic. Yet another reason is that the political interest that has long surrounded Colorni in socialist and democratic circles has not resulted (unfortunately) in a truly profound understanding of his contribution, and the feelings of indignation and emotion that are inevitably evoked by the memory of the Nazi occupation of Rome and Eugenio's tragic end[4] have sometimes overwhelmed the serene (indispensable!) clarity and placidity of the reasoning. And finally, because Colorni's texts from that period, though sharp and illuminating, are few and spare — they seemed insufficient, at least ex

---

[1]Not surprisingly, as I said to Albert when we first met, seeing that I was born a few meters from where Eugenio was shot.

[2]So much so that I wrote in my introduction to Colorni's, *The Discovery of the Possible* (2019, p. 45), that "it does not seem to me appropriate to recall here the extraordinary experience of this versatile and tireless young socialist leader, capable of thinking, teaching, motivating, persuading and writing, as well as taking action. This is not because in speaking of Eugenio's topical politics one might ever consider passing over the bright page of Italian (European and world) history that he wrote in the circumstances. But rather because it has already been re-evoked in ways that cannot be improved upon, by his comrades in arms." This was an involuntary renunciation that I now intend to move beyond.

[3]A key observation by Clifford Geertz (the great anthropologist partner of Albert Hirschman at the School of Social Science of the Institute for Advanced Study beginning in the seventies of the last century) that is especially relevant, in my opinion, in the case of a dramatic and convulsive period like the one we will be dealing with. Only consider that one of the young socialists Colorni knew in such circumstances, the historian Claudio Pavone, managed to bring his thesis of the Resistance as an Italian civil war into the public eye only in 1991.

[4]Tragic from many points of view: personal and collective, cultural and political, Italian and European, and global. . . .

ante, for the creation of a scientifically useful discourse, however partial. Because, because. . . .

The truth is, though, that at certain point a combination of circumstances led me to feel that that the reasoning had reversed itself; that almost unconsciously I had managed to overcome (somewhat recklessly, but with a bit of luck) at least some of these difficulties. My research into his correspondence, the discovery of the possible and the Ventotene dialogues[5] had provided me — indirectly, it seemed — with a starting point for tackling this key issue; and perhaps even a fine thread (Ariadne's?) which I will try to unspool below, as an introduction.

Having realized this, I decided to "try it out" — obviously without any pretense to completeness; moving ahead by degrees, with difficulty and from different angles in seeking to understand Eugenio's last year, and leaving to the reader (especially) the task of glimpsing the main threads of the overall weave of Colorni's fabric, which — as I will argue below — leads in the end to a general interpretive and normative perspective of great value, to be pursued tirelessly, world-wide.

2. Unless I am mistaken, it is not possible to appreciate Eugenio's extraordinary theoretical and practical legacy without fully understanding its political (and personal) aspect — including (it goes without saying) that of the last fiery months of his life. At the same time, however, it is impossible to actually assume such an angle of vision without understanding its intellectual roots.

And yet it is here that we find the "horns of the dilemma" the critics have struggled with for so long. On the one hand, it was decided to publish Colorni's collected writings excluding those that were deemed political.[6] On the other hand, despite the many polit-

---

[5]I refer here to Colorni, *Microfondamenta* (2016) and *La scoperta del possibile. Scritti politici* (2017), and to Colorni and Spinelli, *I dialoghi di Ventotene* (2018) [English tr.: 2019, 2019a, 2020], which I managed to finalize through conversations with Eva Hirschmann for Eugenio's personal aspects, with Mario Quaranta for his relationship with the natural sciences, and with Geri Cerchiai for his philosophy.

[6]In fact, as we know, although Colorni 1975, edited by N. Bobbio carries the title *Scritti* [writings], it does not include those of a political nature, as if these were somehow transitory, or did not in any case rise to the dignity of the publication. In addition, the book had a troubled gestation — originally entrusted to Ferruccio Rossi-Landi it was supposed to have also contained other texts of Eugenio's on the natural sciences which, although already

ical initiatives *about* Eugenio (commemorations, articles, reviews, etc., of which the tireless Leo Solari[7] has long been the deserving protagonist), it cannot be said that the Colorni's political lesson has actually emerged into the light in its true iconoclastic splendor — or even gone beyond the narrow circle of experts.[8]

For this reason, more than seventy years after Eugenio's death (and indirectly protected by this gentlemanly cut-off point[9]) I have tried to prove that things are not, on the whole, as they have thus far been represented to us; without detracting, of course, from the previous work of numerous authors, and indeed drawing (above all) on numerous texts by Solari, the re-issue of the philosophical and autobiographical writings edited by his friend Geri Cerchiai, and the proceedings of the three conferences held on the occasion of the centennial of Colorni's birth.[10]

---

in proof, were omitted in the final version (and still await publication: cf. Degl'Innocenti 2010, p. 37, n. 34, and Quaranta 2011 p. 124). Concerning the title, the "omission" was therefore double. It should also be added that, at least to the present writer, the philosophical interpretation in Norberto Bobbio's introduction has always seemed problematic. (It had to wait more than three decades before encountering the ingenious critical competence of a young scholar – Geri Cerchiai, 2009). With all this, however, it seems to me right to argue that we must be retrospectively grateful to Norberto Bobbio (if only) because he had the courage to break through the delay imposed by the stakeholders — fully thirty years after Eugenio's death.

[7] In 1943–44, as a young socialist leader, Leo Solari was one of Eugenio's closest collaborators.

[8] I am referring, of course, to the many politicians, philosophers, political scientists and historians of the resistance, the workers' movement, etc. who were involved. Perhaps the most significant episode of this intense period of initiatives was the publication of *Eugenio Colorni. Ieri e sempre* [Yesterday and Always] by Leo Solari (1980): "a book," wrote Gaetano Arfé in *Avanti!* 17 July 1980, "that is more a political act than the work of a professional historian or a gesture of devotion to a friend or master." The volume won the Viareggio Presidente Award; and its presentation ceremony included a debate involving Leonida Repaci, Gaetano Arfé, Altiero Spinelli, Giuliano Vassalli, Paolo Ungari, Mario Zagari and Leo Solari, in which, said Arfé and Zagari, "Eugenio is present here among us" (an observation which recalls Albert Hirschman's habit of considering Colorni always present, of talking about him in the present). Nevertheless, this did not lead to more detailed studies. In spite of having announced it, Solari was unable to publish Colorni's political writings. Nor did he succeed in his attempt to assemble a volume of testimony about Colorni (for which he had already written a draft presentation and prepared two sets of questions, one general and the other "personalized," for the Repacis, Manlio Rossi-Doria, Umberto Terracini, Luisa Villani Usellini, and Mario Zagari). Cf. Envelope 1 File 7 of the Solari fund.

[9] I refer to the fact that after that date, by law, it is permitted to publish an author's works without further authorization.

[10] Solari 1980, Colorni 2009, AA.VV. 2010, 2011 and 2011a.

In any case, the point of the pages that follow is not to summarize my short research journey[11] — if only because this "last mile," so to speak, has proved to be anything but simple[12] (I would say, rather: engaging and . . . shocking). If anything, it has been a question of identifying the numerous contradictions scattered in the path ahead in order to learn how to profit from them. Because when one is able to extract meaning from the inevitably fragmentary (and sometimes event-driven) documentation of the daily goings-on of the time, one understands that it contains relevant lessons. For if it is true (unfortunately) that in the course of events in the lives of those (like Luisa Villani Usellini and Leo Solari) who were closest to Eugenio there was *never* sufficient backing to allow Colorni's "good news" to blossom in the progressive culture of the time, it is also true that it has remained in part unexpressed — and even today awaits clarification. Because, while I have the idea that many of the protagonists of that struggle, absorbed as they were in their own narratives, could not find in themselves the necessary humility and perseverance to truly understand "where Eugenio was headed," it also seems to me that there was a logic in that journey that was not in fact incomprehensible. It is simply arduous — first of all due to the difficulty of somehow mastering such a vast and opaque array of materials of all kinds referring to Colorni, and then because of the inalienable necessity — the heart of the matter, really — of offering the reader an informed and as far as possible reliable idea of Eugenio's thoughts and actions.[13]

It is also true that this last requirement has led me to try out unusual pathways, identifying alongside Colorni's writings texts by others that can be connected to him — because they either were published under his responsibility, were (apparently) inspired by him, contain important specific ideas that he shared, or finally, are capable of briefly evoking the overheated atmosphere of the Roman Resistance in which he operated. And yet in the end I had to opt for a

---

[11]Cf. n. 5.

[12]"For us," Eugenio said, "being simple is the most complicated thing there is" (cit. by Leo Solari in "Presentazione per la cosituzione del Circolo Colorni," 8 June 1976: cf. Envelope 1, File of the Solari fund).

[13]Which should also as much as possible reduce overlap and repetition with respect to what has already been published.

fairly obvious solution — to publish in its entirety issue n. 2 of *L'Unità Europea,* under Eugenio's direction, and some of the most significant extracts from the editorials (mainly) from the underground issues of *Avanti!,* for which Colorni had been collaborator, editor, or chief editor, and from the underground paper *La rivoluzione socialista,* the organ of the Socialist Youth Federation, of which Eugenio was "spiritual and political guide."[14]

"To what end?" the perplexed reader will ask. I would answer — to identify and emphasize (directly and indirectly) some "key aspects" of Colorni the federalist and socialist partisan, and to allow these distinctive characteristics to speak to us at such a great distance in time; this in the hope that, spontaneously interacting with each other, they will weave before our eyes a convincing wide-meshed intellectual fabric and will offer us *a political perspective of human civilization* that is attractive, open, and eager to acquire — a little at a time — further contributions.

3. Federalist, socialist, "agitator, journalist, dynamiter, leader of armed bands,"[15] Colorni was a teacher of young revolutionaries and then, as we have seen, drafter, source of inspiration, and editor of several underground publications. My decision was therefore to integrate some of Eugenio's writings with his editorial influence — in both the federalist and socialist camps — as a way of getting closer to other "key aspects" of his experience. In the first place, to the possibilist trajectories that initially, following Colorni, we will indicate (mainly) from below; but which will subsequently be rediscovered (also) from above by Albert Hirschman, Lleras Restrepo, Celso Furtado, Altiero Spinelli, Fernando Henrique Cardoso, and others — to the point of acquiring, at least potentially, a general historical significance.[16]

---

[14]Testimony *in memoriam* of Eugenio's companion, Luisa Villani Usellini, for *La rivoluzione socialista,* June 1944 (now in Colorni 1998, p. 172-73).
[15]Ernesto Rossi *in memoriam* 1944 (now 1975, p. 191).
[16]As seems evident in a famous essay of Albert Hirschman's, "The Search for Paradigms as a Hindrance to Understanding" 1970 (now in Hirschman 1971, p. 342 and ff.), which refers to *Zapata and the Mexican Revolution* by John Womack Jr. (1967).

If all this helps the reader to understand a bit better the last theoretical and practical treasure that Colorni left us, and to think outside the box with respect to murky disciplinary divisions, "principled" political ideologies, and the newsy superficiality of so many of the dramatis personae (including journalism, of course), it will mean that in the end it was worth the effort.

The 12–13 months following the decision to go underground (presumably at the end of April 1943) and its implementation in early May until Eugenio's death (30 May 1944) delimit the temporal arc of Colorni's Roman partisan experience, which in its turn falls spontaneously into three segments of 3–4 months each. The first, dedicated mainly to federalist activity, ran until September 8th and the occupation of the capital by the Nazi-Fascists. The second, Eugenio's federalist and socialist conspiracy of the months that followed, finally culminated without a break in the third, tragic phase — the Nazi-Fascist reaction in the winter and spring of 1944 and the Eugenio's murder a week before the liberation of the capital.

The atmosphere of the first period (sometimes happy — the 25th of July comes to mind, or the first flyer put out by the Resistance on the 26th, or the editorial "Unanimità" [Unanimity] in *L'Unità Europea*) inevitably differed from the heat of what followed, but it was actually in the latter period, many of the protagonists recalled, that Eugenio was able to give his best — in terms of political ideas, everyday life, and action. And it is precisely this hidden miracle that we will try to unveil and bring into focus, not least to offer a broad evaluation of his example and practical politics; and also of their extraordinary meaning — from which we can continue to learn even after such a great span of time.

Of course it must be borne in mind that, prepared as he may have been for an unprecedented task, entirely to be invented, Eugenio inevitably brought with him a gradually-constructed store of intellectual experience that must be understood from other texts. But from the testimony of Luisa Villani Usellini, who became his companion along the way, it emerges that one aspect of Colorni's philosophical thought takes precedence over many others — the theme of love.[17]

---

[17]A brief set of extracts on the subject, coming from various of Eugenio's writings are

A Starting Point

4. Thinking about Colorni's political writings from his final year, what amazes is the extraordinary continuity of inspiration they contain — which certainly did not come *ex-ante* (as a matter of "principle" or ideological choice), but through impassioned participation in the events of the time and daily scrutiny of his own work through Eugenio's habitual practice of reflection, and through the questioning and daily discussion of his theoretical and practical foundations — a sort of mental gymnastics that allowed a step-by-step verification of what he was doing, so that it could be intelligently modified and fitted, glove-like, to the evolving situation.[18]

Thus, the two letters to Altiero Spinelli published below, from May-July 1943, establish certain reference points that crop up later in Colorni's activities and writings as a partisan — both at the end of that year and in the spring of 1944. His admiration for the positive side of Pantagruel (his nickname for Spinelli) in fact re-emerges later in Eugenio's abilities — indeed, his happiness — in a leadership role. The two criticisms he levels at Altiero — mental inertia and ideology — re-emerge in the "Letter to the Ventotene Federalists" from mid-July and in the "Letter to federalist friends in Switzerland" from November 1943 in his need to fully understand the political opportunities offered by developments in the war, and in the reservations he puts forward concerning the young ex-MUPs [Movement for Proletarian Unity] (and again in his two articles in *Avanti!* of March and May 1944).

So Eugenio's political position, which Vassalli would later call that of "a critic and a linchpin,"[19] was already present in this correspondence with Spinelli and found a useful, temporary equilibrium in *L'Unità Europea* 2.[20] It then presented itself again explicitly in Eu-

---

published in English in Colorni 2019, p. 83–89.

[18]This intellectual process of Eugenio's, clarified by Albert Hirschman in a well-known page on their time together in Trieste in 1937–1938 (1995, p. 118–19), was effectively omnipresent in the daily intellectual experience of the two brothers-in-law.

[19]Endowed "with balance and with foresight," Colorni was "a political leader with much greater responsibility than the two authors of the *Manifesto*, 'at once a critic and a linchpin, as Giuliano Vassalli remembered him" (Pasquinucci 2010, p. 297). Cf., below, sec. 27.

[20]Altiero's answer of June 1943 is now in Spinelli 1993. In all probability, this correspondence of May-July 1943 was intended for clandestine distribution by the Federalist Move-

genio's socialist conspiracy — in the form of a challenge to the leadership of the PSIUP [Socialist Party for Proletarian Unity] alongside
the younger socialists and (at the same time) as a way of channeling
the political energy of these young people within the Party.

Of course, the Roman Resistance did not represent the decisive
turning point that Eugenio perhaps believed it would,[21] perhaps due
to the optical effect typical of great social upheavals that make something appear to be imminent when it actually needs time to unfold.
And yet it cannot be denied that, along with the Four days of Naples,
it was the forerunner of a great national saga that heralded Italy's
post-war recovery and the launch of the construction of Europe;
and that the subsequent political process unfolded over time partly
in the way that Eugenio had glimpsed in 1943, under a rationale that
surprisingly was picked up and has been followed ever since.

This being the case, Eugenio's lesson actually appears to be
foundational: in humanistic and scientific culture, in the social sciences, and in democratic politics — probably far beyond what he
himself would have imagined. And it is precisely this "key" aspect
of the whole story that (as we shall see) draws us into the searing
atmosphere of Colorni's last year.

5. At the beginning of his letter of May 1943, Eugenio expressed
his deep admiration and sympathy for Altiero Spinelli's 'Pantagruelian' attitude — of "the entertainer, the teacher, the person who exudes warmth, who only needs to appear and people will follow him."
Thereafter, he himself would in part follow in these footsteps. But
the point is that this attitude was not enough.[22] "You have planted

---

ment, in a booklet entitled *The Practical Implementation of European Unity. A Discussion
between Federalists* (See below, Eugenio's hints at this in the "Letter to the Ventotene Federalists"). But then, although prepared for printing, the texts (somewhat condensed) of the
three letters were not published (see Spinelli 1993, p. 190, n.) — perhaps due to the overlap-
ping of the events that followed and (/or) because, since a balance between the two authors
was arrived at in *L'Unità Europea* 2 the leaflet was no longer considered indispensable.

[21]So that he wrote (in the "Letter to Federalist Friends in Switzerland" in November 1943,
cf. below): "my impression is that the political configuration in Italy over the next months
will be decided when the English get to Rome."

[22]"You started out assuming that at the end of the war the floodgates are suddenly going to
open and the waters will rush down and submerge everything. And you assigned to yourself and whoever follows you the task of digging the great channel that will guide these

yourself in the middle of the current," Eugenio argues, speaking directly to Altiero, "you've built your embankments, and now you're surprised that so little water is swirling between them. [. . .] But the fact is that [. . .] the waters are rapidly opening channels further down [. . .]. But you don't notice. [Y]our 'Pantagruelian' way [. . .] makes you fall into errors of perspective and make blunders — that's all."

But there is more: "The second thing I want to reproach you for," Eugenio continues, "is not so much a personal defect as having let yourself be dragged, almost in spite of yourself, into a sin that is very common among those forced to practice politics in prison, confinement or exile. It is what I would call the sin of 'ideology,'" what prompts many to seek "the right dosages" of "freedom and authority, socialism and democracy, etc. [. . .] You too want to give the word socialism its most correct and modern definition; you too are preparing your socialist sauce seasoned with liberalism to enter in the competition with the others."

Eugenio then draws from this a generalization — that, like philosophy, "so also politics, in my view, will not move forward by retouching its ideological structure, setting out the formulations and solutions for eternal problems; but *by keeping its eye on developing events and trying to influence them using the most effective and unbiased methods*; always, of course, in the light of some basic positions which it should be enough to have clear in one's heart and, I would say, in one's instincts."[23]

We arrive at the point. "The victorious nations of the last war," Eugenio declared, "tried to dominate the defeated states through territorial mutilation, military restrictions, economic and financial burdens. But they were not remotely concerned with influencing domestic politics. Germany, Austria, Turkey, Greece, and Italy were left in the grip of their own internal upheavals [. . .]. Now I don't

---

waters and make them once again beneficial and fertile. In effect, this is what happened in many European countries in 1918." But this situation will not necessarily repeat itself. "What if," Eugenio asks, "tomorrow's postwar period doesn't present this fluid and chaotic aspect, this new primordial state where victory is there to be seized by whoever has the most open mind and the stoutest heart?" His first objection is thus that Altiero doesn't explore possible alternatives; he doesn't consider the actual range of concrete possibilities.
[23]Italics mine.

know how the winners will treat the losers at the end of this war. But one thing I do know for sure — this time they will not make the mistake of staying out of domestic politics. Intentions are very clear on this point; and not a day goes by when they are not reaffirmed by all parties involved. They want to destroy the fascist regimes once and for all, and no resurgence of nationalisms, chauvinisms, etc. will be countenanced. [. . .] This time we are in the presence of two very powerful state organizations that present themselves as paladins of the two basic ideologies contending for the European field. Fighting for one of these ideologies will mean, not only implicitly but in the general consciousness of the people, fighting in favor of the corresponding power. The communism-democracy antithesis has gradually transformed itself into a Russia-England "antithesis."[24]

"It is by now clear," he continues further on, "that once the two areas of influence have been established, the whole postwar period will be dominated by an open or covert struggle between the victorious powers, by the attempted expansion of one at the expense of the other, and by their efforts to take control of key positions. The site of this struggle will be the continent of Europe, and clearly the people of Europe will not remain passive. On the contrary, the character of the contest will depend to a great extent on them — whether it will burn itself out in a simple imperialist clash between Russia and England, or whether it will be the starting point for the effective unification of the continent. One way or the other, what emerges from this perspective is that the struggle for European unity will no longer be limited to the narrow time frame between the end of hostilities and the conclusion of the peace [as we believed at Ventotene[25]],

---

[24]Obviously, in their debates, the Ventonene federalists were not yet able to foresee or even imagine the dominant role that the United States would have in the second post-war period. "Our illusions about England," he belatedly recognized with a hint of self-irony, referring to himself and Ernesto Rossi (Spinelli 1984, p. 317), "were hardly less than Colorni's about Russia. Strangely enough, the United States, whose constitutional structure had seemed so important to us that we had been ready to propose it as a model for Europe, didn't break into our Eurocentric vision except as little more than an appendage of England."

[25]"Two years ago," Eugenio had written moments earlier, "when we were thinking about the unity of Europe, it presented itself as a goal to be reached in a single leap, in the period immediately after the cessation of hostilities. 'It is essential,' we said, 'that we not wait for the hot lava to re-solidify in the old molds. We need to strike while the iron is hot, and see to it that when the victors sit down at the peace conference table to give Europe a new ori-

but will have at its disposal the broader postwar period. The last two years, I believe, have brought about this change in our prospects and made them vastly more concrete and feasible than they were before."

Am I awake or dreaming? I had to rub my eyes and reread this paragraph several times before I understood what it contained (and contains). Instead of feeling crushed, torn up by the interactive logic of the two opposing superpowers, Eugenio had glimpsed here, with certain intuition, the emergence of a *possibilist opportunity*: a step that on its own moved wagon-loads of theory into the attic. . . .

6. "The two winning states, each the arbiter of a piece of our continent," Colorni goes on to write, "have two paths open to them. One is a policy of housekeeping, of internal reconstruction, reinforcing the ruling class, repaying their own people for their sacrifices during the war by improving their economic conditions and promoting their psychological position as 'winners'; keeping the countries in their own sphere of influence in a state of economic and military semi-subjugation, covertly sabotaging any real revolutionary effort they might make, any attempt to clean house to make way for renewal. Or, there is the other path — joining with the vanquished, constituting with them a true and deeply-rooted unity; absorbing their lifeblood and civilizing forces; reconstructing together, sharing power with their ruling classes and letting them participate in leading the new unity being created; and facing the other half of Europe as a compact, aggressive bloc, endowed with an immensely strong power of popular attraction."

Instead of a predetermined perspective, there would thus be a choice — at the level of great-power governments, to be sure, but also at the popular level. "The two winners," Colorni writes, "will oscillate continually between these two extremes. From a purely nationalistic point of view, the first option would represent a reinforcement of nationalist structures and would safeguard them against yesterday's enemies; but the second would allow very active

---

entation, they find before them a Europe already launched on the road to unification by the revolutionary strength of its people. If we can't seize this chance at the opportune moment, we will have lost it forever; and the unification of Europe will have to be put off until the end of the Third World War.'"

and independent policy choices vis-a-vis the other winner, which would be prevented from extending its tentacles into the first winner's sphere of influence to try to break it up and win it over. Even imperialist aims, broadly intended, might be advanced for either of the two victorious powers by a European policy. But certainly a decisive element in determining the choice is the concrete situation that is created in the countries within their spheres of influence. [. . .] In short, *it is in the power of the peoples of Europe to force the winning powers to come out of their nationalistic shell and to set in motion, even in spite of themselves, a policy of European unification."*

This is the point of view that Colorni resolutely held during the intense Roman months that followed, right up to his last writings — awaiting a revolution with a German epicenter (which never happened), but at the same time actively preparing for the arrival of the Allied troops. . . .

The people, he wrote, "can see to it that the situation breaks [. . .]. This is the high card in their hands. A card that will need to be played in actions involving the masses; not based on abstract federalist ideology, but rather stressing something people will be more than ready for — the fact that it is their attitude, every time, that can decide the outcome of a particular development in international politics, moving it in one direction or the other[26] [. . .].

"From what I've said," Eugenio concluded, "you can deduce what I think of the 'European Federalist Movement.' While participating wholeheartedly in the pursuit of its avowed purpose, I charge it with the defect of building the model of the perfect European federation too carefully, forgetting to observe the many outcomes of the drastic moves made by the countless forces on today's political chessboard — outcomes which, though sometimes following unexpected paths that we could hardly have imagined, have served our own purposes. Only if we have the openness to recognize these formidable forces, and to embed our activity in their framework, only then will we get out of the field of noble ideology and into that of concrete action."

---

[26]It is, he wrote, "like the action of the men of the Risorgimento, who organized uprisings and movements all over the peninsula for the purpose of provoking intervention and making sure the international situation would come down on the side of Italian Unity."

The Roman Federalist Commitment

7. This is not the place to discuss the specifics of the correspondence between Eugenio and Altiero[27] (also marked by conjectures about future developments in the situation). It is enough to point out that in spite of a certain narrowing of the gap between them,[28] Eugenio at first maintained that his political differences with Spinelli would make their collaboration difficult. But later, as work with his Ventotene friends developed, he reconsidered.[29] He took on the leadership of the Roman federalist group and the newspaper; and he began to believe that if federalism had taken the form of a movement (rather than the party supported by the *Ventotene Manifesto*[30]), the coexistence and collaboration between different points of view would have benefited greatly, so that the federalists could have represented a wide range of orientations, open to a variety of political experiences — from the pro-Westerners who favored the Action Party, to the socialists themselves.[31]

---

[27]It is a debate in which industrious readers who so desire can "immerse themselves" personally: cf. above, n. 20. (My comments on this are in Colorni 2019a, p. 29–34.)

[28]As Altiero in fact answered in June 1943 (1993, p. 203), "I was pleased with the way your letter showed me that developing events have brought our viewpoints closer together," although they nevertheless remained rather apart.

[29]In fact, in his "Letter to the Ventotene federalists," signed "*Commodus* (Aldo from now on)" [his signature on the Ventotene dialogues, replaced from then on by Aldo], "Dear friends, At the conclusion of a nearly plenary session it was decided that I should take over the direction of the movement. I hope to discharge my function to everyone's satisfaction. Our last discussions had caused me to fear that our shortcomings were too serious to allow us collaborate productively. But the articles you have sent, which I agree with almost completely [. . .], clearly show that you also think the tone of the newspaper should be such that both our points of view are entitled to citizenship. This is the advantage of being a movement and not a political party."

[30]Spinelli and Rossi 1944; now in Spinelli 1985, p. 35–37.

[31]"The leadership is constituted as follows," he wrote, listing its members in their diverse functions (editing the newspaper, press distribution, relations with people and parties, and with Ventotene and Milan, secretarial work, etc). "Naturally," he specified, "these duties are flexible and can be shifted according to the occasion and need." "In the spring of 1943," Cerilo Spinelli confirmed, "what could be defined as the first directorate of the European federalist movement already existed, composed of Eugenio Colorni, Guglielmo Usellini, Ursula Hirschmann and Cerilo Spinelli. 'This Committee had never been elected by anyone because we were underground at the time and the federalist movement had no popular base, but we felt that we were the interpreters of Altiero ad Ernesto's thinking, firstly because we were in fairly frequent contact, considering that we were underground — Altiero would recall the wooden boxes that moved between Rome and Ventotene, whose false bottoms concealed messages and news — and also because we had with us Eugenio

On 6 May 1943, on the pretext of a radiology appointment in
Potenza, Colorni fled his confinement at Melfi and went underground.[32] Furthermore, the Eugenio covertly making his way toward Rome was no longer (obviously) the young and enterprising
history and philosophy teacher from the Giosuè Carducci Institute
in Trieste who, assisted by his attractive wife (Ursula Hirschmann),
had led a sparkling social life, not least as a cover for his anti-fascist
activities; no longer was he the director of the internal Socialist Center, able to navigate between some activities in the light of day and
others underground; no longer the author of enlightening political
articles published abroad. Because for nearly five years he had suffered the mortification of prison and confinement.

Even under such unhappy conditions (aggravated by repeated
crises of depression), Eugenio had held up — he had undertaken
long-term, systematic studies of the natural sciences (mainly math-
ematics and physics) on one hand, and philosophy, literature, psychology and psychoanalysis on the other. He had written autobiographical and philosophical texts of great value. Along with Altiero
Spinelli, Ernesto Rossi, Ursula Hirschmann and a small group of internees, he had taken part in the discovery of a political idea he considered crucial — the federalist idea of European unity. And now, in
his early maturity, resuming an active political life armed with the
concept of love (as mentioned above), he burned with the desire to
put into practice the key political ideas on European unity discussed
at such length at Ventotene.

In Rome, Colorni was at first the guest of Guglielmo Usellini
and Luisa Villani Usellini, who were already part of a small federalist circle, drawn together during the previous two years by Ursula

---

and Ursula Colorni who had witnessed and participated in the birth and development of
federalist thinking and positions'" (cit. in Rognoni Vercelli 1991, p. 85).

[32]According to Antonio Tedesco (2014, p. 150), "These were months in which the stiff
shirts of the regime began to fray and the loyalty of peripheral officials begins to falter."
"His escape was possible," declared Ada Rossi, Ernesto's wife, "because, contrary to what
usually happened, he was not accompanied to Potenza by the carabinieri, and he managed
to get on the train that took him to Rome." At the same time, "two letters addressed to his
wife Ursula in Melfi with Spanish postage stamps and censorship stamps, led the Ministry
of the Interior to inform Foreign Affairs that Colorni had probably taken refuge in Spain —
in Madrid. But it was an act of deliberate misdirection" (Bumbaca 2004, p. 46).

and Ada Rossi, the extraordinary message carriers between Ventotene and the mainland.[33] "Within a few days," wrote Ernesto Rossi
in memoriam,[34] "he managed to publish *L'Unità Europea,* construct
the first federalist group in Rome, distribute typescripts of the texts
we had sent from Ventotene, and re-establish relations with our
friends at various confinement centers and cities of Italy. I remember our joy at extracting from beneath the false bottom of a box
duly searched by the police the first issue[35] of *L'Unità Europea.* We

---

[33]Eugenio "had turned up at my house [at viale Gorizia 52] in May of 1943 in a highly ner-
vous state," wrote Guglielmo Usellini to Willi Schwartz, Eugenio's brother-in-law (cf. *L'avvenire dei Lavoratori,* S. Merli, ed., Istituto Europeo Studi Sociali, Milano 1992). "He was
in flight from confinement and perhaps a bit from himself as well. But he had a very clear intuition about what was coming. At the time many thought his action was rash. But I accepted
it." Following this, according to the testimony of Ada Rossi (Solari fund, Envelope 1, File
23), Colorni was the guest of Bruno Visentini, found a room to rent, and occasionally slept
with his Pontecorvo relatives at via Livorno 25. Finally, he moved for several months to the
home of Sirio Lentini, medical pathology assistant at the Policlinico, probably through the
intercession of Altiero's mother who was a friend of Sirio's. Eugenio moved around Rome
"using the identity card of a Polish doctor." He felt alive, "freed from the conditions of pe-
rennial inactivity" he had been condemned to in confinement. According to the testimony of
Sirio Lentini, "he was excited about his political struggle and the federalist idea." Eugenio
and Sirio "slept in the same room and a sincere friendship was was born between them; the
professor got him a Policlinico library card and on a number of occasions helped him hide
newspapers and mimeographed materials in the rooms and basements of the Policlinico.
Lentini was not entirely aware of Colorni's movements and activities inside the antifascist
opposition, recalling that Colorni went out in the morning and returned in the evening, often
with newspapers and leaflets." (Solari fund, Envelope 1, File 13).

[34]Rossi 1944, now 1975, p. 190. "This contrast — the contrast between Eugenio Colorni
the intellectual and the political activist that a deep moral need had led him to become —
makes his heroic life stand out all the more." Ibid., p. 192.

[35]Actually, it was the second issue. N. 1, of May 1943, had been "put to bed" in Milan at
a meeting attended by Alberto and Guido Rollier, Giorgio Payronel and Ursula Hirschman
(cf. Rognoni Vercelli 1991, p. 86). It contained, under the masthead, the following banner
headline: "At the end of this war the unification of Europe will stand as a possible and
essential task. The division of Europe into nation-states is today the worst enemy of the
humane formulation and solution of our problems. The external threat, fantastic or real,
upends all processes and has opened the way for the ridiculous march of all kinds of reactionary forces towards the absurdity and war of the last seventy years." This same edition
of *Unità Europea* contained an editorial on the federalist movement which, after speaking
of "Anguish," "The European federalist solution" and "Our action," concluded: "We seek
the death of provincial, nationalist Italy, closed to Europe, to allow the resurrection of
a free and open Italy within a united Europe. Like Mazzini and Cattaneo, 'we love our
country because we love all countries.'" In a handwritten manuscript note of Altiero's on
the copy of the newspaper kept in the Fiesole archive of the European Institute, Ursula is
credited with bringing that issue of the newspaper to completion.

finally had our newspaper! Eugenio had been exemplary."[36]

Moreover, the situation was favorable, mainly due to the decline of fascism which, following the allied landing in Sicily, would culminate in the fall of Mussolini (25 July). This event without doubt presented an extraordinary political opportunity (unfortunately ephemeral[37]). But it was also an important intellectual opportunity, which allowed Colorni to publish an underground issue of *L'Unità Europea* that was of great interest — n. 2.[38] Even after so many years it still stands, in my opinion as one of the most convincing, explicit and authoritative expressions of the European (and beyond) federalist perspective — even by comparison with the better-known *Manifesto*.

8. Following Eugenio's intentions,[39] the four main articles that make up this issue of *L'Unità Europea* ("August 1943, Voice of the European Federalist Movement") — that is, the editorial "Unanimity," "Character of the European Federation," "Movement or Party?" and "Federalist Tendencies" — should be read as parts of a single line of reasoning (even though they were undoubtedly written by different hands).[40] In addition, in my opinion, in focusing on the

---

[36]Rossi 1944, now 1975, p. 190. There is a small puzzle here that needs to be solved. How is it possible that this actually happened when, as the reader can check in person (see below), the first page of that newspaper reads: "At the moment of going to press we have received news of the liberation of ERNESTO ROSSI, RICCARDO BAUER and VINCENZO CACACE." We know, on the other hand, that Ernesto's release took place in July. It therefore seems plausible to speculate that in Regina Coeli, where he had been moved on 7 July, Ernesto did not receive a copy of the newspaper, but a "printer's proof."

[37]The popular will to eliminate fascism from the life of the nation, according to the underground *Avanti!* (n. 8, p. 2), "had already shown itself openly following 25 July, during the brief interval when the police measures of the Badoglio government allowed it."

[38]Reading and rereading the small and precise texts, without a single word out of place, printed in minute but neat characters on both sides of two pages (like a "foolscap sheet"), it is easy to forget that we are really looking at an underground issue of *Unità Europea*. It is as if the sobriety of the words used were competing with that of the tiny spaces, the unexpected effect being to give greater prominence to their important content.

[39]In his "Letter to the Ventotene Federalists," he wrote that "[w]e can give the newspaper a generic character without going into the details of [. . .] questions [we have] among ourselves." Consequently, the articles we will now discuss represent jointly and severally, in my opinion, the point of view of the federalist movement at that period of time — a temporary but successful balance between its components.

[40]The editorial, prompted (obviously) by the events of 25 July, took the place of the "initial brief on the action" Eugenio had mentioned in the "Letter to the Ventotene Federalists" in mid-July (cf. below). Furthermore, in all probability, "Character of the European Federa-

points that interest us most, we should alternate between two frames of interpretation, one with reference to the time when they were written, and the other from the vantage point of today — because in some ways, as we shall see, they are in hindsight still significant.[41] First and foremost, the second issue of *L'Unità Europea* contains an extraordinary editorial, in all probability written by Eugenio, that speaks of popular *unanimity* (never truer, deeper or more heartfelt than following 25 July); of a *vox populi* that could not be ignored and that demanded in one voice "Peace, out with the Nazis, liberty!" But a careful reading reveals that the author's sense of responsibility would not let him be carried away by a movement that was in that particular moment truly overwhelming. Along with the unforgettable explosions of joy and enthusiasm and rediscovered expressions of sincerity and trust, he in fact detected the existence of a lost and uncertain mass of people wondering whom they should obey. They were at a crossroads — between peace and war, between Germany and the United Nations, between fascism and freedom. There was an immediate political need to resolve these dualities quickly and correctly, focusing on the powerful voice of the people and moving without hesitation to satisfy their simple and crucial aspirations. The sooner this happened, he concluded, the stronger the voice of the new Italy would be, and the more comprehensive would be its right to take part in the building of a free and united Europe.

---

tion" was, in the letter, "your article on Churchill's speech," and had therefore been written at Ventotene. "Movement or Party?" was "an article [probably editorial, perhaps written by Guglielmo Usellini] entitled 'Movement or Party?'" Finally "Federalist Tendencies," also apparently an editorial (to which Eugenio perhaps contributed), took the place of "the publication of federalist statements sent to us by various Italian and foreign sources" (the first issue of the paper had been dedicated to statements in favor of federalism from Count Sforza's letter to the Italian people, the platforms of the Action Party, the Movement for Proletarian Unity, and the Social Labor Party, the manifesto of Liberal-Socialism, Pius XII's Christmas message, the Orientations of the Italian Democratic Movement, Fortnightly, and the Lausanne Gazette). Finally, "an article on the dissolution of the Communist International" and "your [Ventotene's] critique of the PdA [Action Party] program, though planned, were in the end not published.

[41]This is in essence a mental experiment which, as Eugenio taught us, inevitably contains an element of subjectivity that cannot be eliminated. So, while I allow myself to set out my own interpretation of these texts, I invite readers to work out, in their own hearts if you will . . . readings of their own.

But which Europe should it be? We shall seek the answer in an exploration of the article that follows, entitled "Character of the European Federation."[42] The Ventotene group, like the embryonic Roman Federalist movement we are talking about, had no notion of the role the United States would play at the end of the war[43] — the axis powers' main western antagonist was Great Britain; and the main theater of operations was still Europe (which, in their view, would in any case keep its central role in the life and economy of the planet even after the war). Accordingly, the article begins by citing Winston Churchill's speech of 21 April on the new international order. And after declaring "along with all English people with European sensibilities," that they could not say that they were satisfied with the current state of affairs the writers continued as follows:

> When we talk about European unity, we mean a great and complex movement of spiritual, political and economic forces whose task over the course of the next few decades will be to bring different peoples together in a common effort of civilization that will erase the nightmare of new wars on the continent. For this vision to be more than a vague ideal, however, it is essential that we be aware of the need for an adequate international structure — and for this, even if it is not at present possible to set out all the details, it is necessary to have its fundamental features clearly in mind, or else the goal will not be achieved.[44]

So there is a declared purpose — the bringing together of the European peoples "in a common effort of civilization." There is at the same time the need for "an adequate international structure" to be able to achieve that purpose. Clearly, the article says, these

---

[42]This article was attributed to Colorni by Karl Voigt, who edited the English language edition. Cf. Voigt, "Ideas of the Italian Resistance on the Postwar Order in Europe," with the English translation of "Character of the European Federation" in the appendix (p. 506–08): in Walter Lipgens, ed., *Documents on the History of European Integration*, De Guyter, Berlin-New York, 1985, vol. 1. In any case, it is clear from the text and the accompanying notes that it is only a hypothesis — and one that is furthermore contradicted apertis verbis by the "Letter to the Ventotene Federalists": cf., above, n. 40.

[43]As I have mentioned: cf. above, n. 24.

[44]Italics ours.

two elements are connected in a one-to-one correspondence, in the sense that without the second, the first will fail.[45] And not only that, says the article: following the same logic, the reverse would also be true — it would make no sense, that is, to conceive the fundamental features of "an adequate international structure" if the goal of the brotherhood of European peoples were not pursued as well.

This leads to a first, surprising conclusion. Reading this passage today, more than seventy-five years later, it is immediately clear that (from a certain point onward) the post-war trajectory of our construction of Europe must have (at least partly) gone off the rails, "lost its bearings," even if — it must be added — it could still find them again. In other words it was not able to go beyond a certain point in the unification of the peoples of Europe as a general alternative to the rebirth of nationalism; and it would truly have to commit itself in this direction if it really intended to get back on track. Even the key goal of the brotherhood of the European peoples has disappeared from sight, replaced in the current eloquence of politicians and officials by the simple pursuit of peace, and then by the ideology of "counting" — of being a "global player" in international forums.[46]

9. On the other hand, this rather shocking first impression is further articulated and consolidated in the next paragraph — in what it

---

[45]This is reminiscent of *National Power*, the book Albert Hirschman had by then written in far-off California and which he published in 1945. The book in fact argues for the need to control the sovereignty of states at an international level to stop their continuing to manipulate foreign trade to their advantage, especially when it involves smaller and poorer countries. Such advocacy in itself provides a glimpse of possible interaction, for objective reasons, between initiatives from below (à la Colorni) and from above (à la Hirschman).

[46]This is a point of view that has been repeated a thousand times in recent years, but which is surely improper, not to say spurious, from the Ventotene point of view as well as from that of the Roman beginnings of the Federalist Movement. The fact is, even from an economic point of view, it is *brotherhood* that must lead us to superior results in terms of productivity such as to encourage in turn the further growth of this same feeling of unity — while this will not happen if the process fails to occur, slackens off or is actually reversed. In other words, the ideology of "counting," being a "global player" without (or even at the expense of) brotherhood contains in itself the nationalist virus that promotes the expansion of systemic internal and external international hierarchies; and, as we see on a daily basis, does not lead even to the essential unleashing of productive energies. The result is that the alternative of federalism vs nationalism is reproduced even in the evolution of the economy, and once again offers the choice of two possible roads — federalist or nationalist.

says as well as suggests: "The tasks of the [European] federation must consist essentially of guaranteeing international peace, ensuring free political life to all countries, abolishing economic autarchies and preventing them from being re-established, determining a single international currency, and abolishing colonial empires — that is, the exclusive possession by some powers of territories rich in raw materials."

More than a first step (as it appears to be in the *Ventotene Manifesto*[47]), European federal unity thus appeared to those who drafted this text as *the "linchpin" of a possible general transition* which, from a system supported by nationalist rivalries (and therefore dangerously unstable, even from a political/military standpoint, as the two world wars had demonstrated *ad abundantium*) would instead lead to a federalist system of general brotherhood which, as such, would be much more stable, responsible, socially just, committed to guaranteeing peace, etc.[48] European unity would trigger a sort of unitary federalist process on a global scale. The purpose, in the words of Carlo Cattaneo, would become the *civilizing of humanity*.[49]

"To properly carry out this task," the article continues, "a federation — that is, a political unit that allows free peoples to participate in community life and does not constitute the veiled or flagrant hegemony of one state over all the others — must be founded on a basic principle [. . .]: *the federation cannot be a league among states. It has to be a res publica of all Europeans.* [. . .] The degree to which we achieve it [this objective] will depend on the degree to which we move away from imperialist forms and power-balance politics and move toward the principle of free cooperation among civilized peoples."

---

[47]More precisely, the *Manifesto* (Spinelli and Rossi 1944; now in Spinelli 1985 p. 30) proposes as its "main duty the creation of a solid international state [. . .] to bring about international unity," but then, in the succeeding paragraph, argues that "now is the time to put down the foundations for a movement capable of mobilizing all forces to build the new organism which will be the grandest, most innovative creation in Europe for centuries." And all the other continents?

[48]"In Colorni's vision of the European cause," recalled Leo Solari (2004, p. 20), "specific elements concerning the 'Manifesto' were recognizable in the impressions we drew from his words. [. . .] He argued that it couldn't just be a question of eliminating the borders between the peoples of our continent. The federalist design needed to be universalist in its scope."

[49]Here we see the broadest and most general expression of Eugenio's ideas on love.

Abolishing nationalism therefore meant suppressing the relations of domination between states (and presumably also within each of them[50]); and above all it meant, as far as possible, achieving "*a res publica, a commonwealth of all Europeans,* who must," the text goes on to explain, "through their direct representatives and not through state ministries, contribute to the determination of the federal will; they must make contributions directly, and not through their state treasuries, to cover federal expenses; they must be called upon directly, and not through state armed forces, to form a militia for the maintenance of order in the federation; and finally, they must be responsible to federal powers for any infraction of federal law. In short, what must be created is real European citizenship — that is, a direct link of rights and duties between the federation and federated citizens."

European Citizenship

10. Agreed. But does it make sense, the reader might object at this point (with a hint of malicious irony) to return to a step like this today, in the face of the incontrovertible historical fact that this hoped-for "leap" from one system to another has not proved possible?

In my view it does make sense — in the face of the current regurgitation of nationalism both within and outside Europe. It makes sense if the basic principle is interpreted not as a *sine qua non,* but as a progressive trend to be pursued systematically and unceasingly.

It absolutely makes sense — as an antidote, first of all, to the oblivion that brotherhood (along with the civilizing process) has fallen into, as we have just seen. This is a key goal which, not by chance, is currently (and dangerously) being neglected. Because the fact is, this is the (only) perspective from which the basic principle of *a res publica of all Europeans* actually makes sense as a pole star for fed-

---

[50]It is a question that torments us as Italians. The lucky thing, however, is that 1) down through the ages, Milan's domination of our country has never entirely succeeded (and nor will it now, it appears, in spite of the evident pretensions of many of its inhabitants); 2) Italy today neither dominates nor intends to, either internally or externally; and 3) this obvious quality of our country's of "not frightening anyone" implicitly gives us a competitive advantage on a global level — one that is much more important than it might seem at first sight — which we should learn to take advantage of. . . .

eralist action, a concrete alternative to be pursued in the face of the
unfortunately possibility of an imminent unleashing of nationalistic
and imperialist rivalries on a European and/or global scale. . . .

It has now been some time since we lost sight of both the aim
and the basic principle of European unity, and we are acutely aware
not only that disorientation is widespread, but also that this may
represent a danger, present and future. And we even wonder about
a concern, or a distressing premonition perhaps, expressed by Eugenio and his friends at Ventotene[51] in an analogy between what
had just happened and the third war of independence during the
Italian Risorgimento. That is to say, we wonder whether, in order to
come to its senses, humanity will not in the end have to go through
a third terrifying world war. . . .

Thinking about it, the advantage we have now, as compared
with a few years ago, is that the theme has actually reappeared on
its own. Before this happened, the *urbi et orbi* resurgence of nationalism in the West had been growing gradually behind the scenes.
For a long time it represented a sort of "malaise" whose nature we
were unable even to diagnose — in a certain sense it had forced our
thinking to proceed within its own frame of reference.

Now, on the other hand, it has exploded into the open, and
this also allows us in hindsight to understand *why*[52] the European
landscape had been clouding over — why, for example, we have
long suffered from the euro and from restrictive economic policies.
Could it not have been the gradual assertion of the "veiled [and/] or
flagrant hegemony of one state over all the others"? Is it not perhaps
the case that the process of progressive "hegemonization" has un-
dermined collective trust in Europe over time, not least thanks to
the marginalization and impoverishment (relative as well as absolute) of numerous countries, territories and social strata, especially

---

[51]In a passage from a letter from Eugenio to Altiero of May 1943 (cf. above, n. 25) that, as
we shall see, is substantially represented in "Federalist Tendencies."

[52]Both in Europe and in the United States, through a sort of social and electoral uprising
with jingoist roots (this is the original Victorian term) which involved large working-class,
rural, suburban, and marginalized areas characterized by a low degree of education. Suddenly we found ourselves re-reading, in everyday reality, *The War in South Africa* (1900),
The Psychology of Jingoism (1901) and *Imperialism* (1902) by John A. Hobson.

the poorest? And isn't it precisely this process which, accelerated by the extremely dangerous Middle Eastern fuse (migration included), has led all these populisms to "detonate"?

In other words, if we are not able to clearly and vigorously re-establish the line of demarcation, both within and outside our populations and countries, that sets democratic federalism apart from nationalism, we will very soon find ourselves disarmed in the face of the imminent future evolution of the planet, which, unfortunately, promises to be anything but auspicious.[53]

11. "What must be created," continues "Character of the European Federation," "is real European citizenship — that is, a direct bond of rights and duties between the federation and federated citizens. Just as today, along with being citizens of our towns we are citizens of the state [. . .] tomorrow we will be actual citizens of the European federation. This is essential, because only by applying this principle will we be able to create an organism that will allow the formation of widespread European consciousness. Today there is no such widespread consciousness, and a federation will only become viable if it is designed in a way that will favor its development. But to achieve this it is essential that within the sphere of federal functions, the wall of national states should be breached."

We can apply such reasoning to ourselves — as I have observed — only by translating it into a gradual evolutionary process. So if it is true, then, that the progress of the federation allows the formation of a widespread European consciousness, it is also true that the latter, over time, will in turn allow federal advances.[54] At the same time, experience also shows that steps forward by one or the other of these can be followed by setbacks — the road is by no means linear or to be taken for granted. It is clear, in fact, that both feder-

---

[53]As I see it, this is a reason (of great current interest) why it has suddenly become *even more* meaningful to work on the thought and action of Eugenio Colorni and his federalist "circle." Because, if we make ourselves aware of the sense of perspective implicit in the alternatives before us today, we can act more consciously. The situation — as numerous authors in fact warn us — would require us to fight the revival of nationalism openly, and to move forward with European (and worldwide, I would add) construction. . . .

[54]As we shall see below (cf. sec. 12), this reasoning requires a change of emphasis with respect to the dictates of this issue of *L'Unità Europea* that, especially in "Federalist Tendencies" understandably stresses the federation-consciousness relation, rather than its opposite.

alist construction and European consciousness must be achieved
through repeated efforts and constant pressure, always illuminat-
ed by brotherhood, free cooperation, and the communal task of
civilizing, and by the European *res publica* — as an alternative to
resurgent nationalisms and their claims of domination.[55]

In conclusion, "the idea that establishing a federation means
creating federal citizenship must be *the compass*[56] that in the future
leads us to accept viable solutions, whatever name they go by, and
to reject those that, while perhaps prestigious in appearance, would
be absolutely unsuited to development in the direction we want."
This conclusion is of great interest, because — as I realized at this
point (with some amazement) — arguing the need for a *compass* to
distinguish between valid and invalid solutions, the text implicitly
recognizes that even at that time the latter represented an impend-
ing danger.[57] Proof of this is that the column "Federalist Tendencies," which completes the newspaper, includes "a note of clarification" concerning certain anti-fascists who, out of convenience, tact,
or lack of conviction, "speak or write about it [federalism] without
giving due emphasis to its importance," and continue to display "an
attitude that is still confused and distrustful."[58]

---

[55]The same may be said of the section that follows (which also, for those familiar with
these issues, has a penetrating whiff of déjà vu). "A federal political body consisting of an
assembly of state delegates," it begins, "would ensure that federal problems continued to
be worked out and decided in the closed space of state ministries, within the purview of the
overall interests of this or that state. Nationalist groups would thus face each other compact, jealous, and wary. The voices you would hear would still be those of Italy, Germany,
and France, and never those of the European classes of Italians, Germans, and Frenchmen
who on many occasions might find themselves in greater agreement with each other than
with their respective countrymen on certain questions. State representation consolidates
national narrow-mindedness, while direct representation helps create an international political life that is truly national and no longer a diplomatic game." A line of reasoning that the
article further exemplifies, speaking of taxation and European "armed forces."
[56]Italics ours.
[57]To be opposed by a movement rather than a party — this is the thesis of the third article
in this issue of *Unità Europea,* which I return to below — cf. sec. 15.
[58]"For example: they do not say that the resolution of the problem in a federal direction
constitutes the *sine qua non* for any further progress and for the salvation of Western civilization; they do not assert, as they should, that the best-designed economic and social
constitutional reforms within the scope of single nation-states would be sand castles if the
European states failed to come together in a solid federal pact. [. . .] This being the case,
it is easy to see why on this subject they fall back on careful, moderate, non-committal
formulas that anyone could subscribe to. [. . .] They recognize the need for an overhaul of

12. Thus, in explicit disagreement with anyone who considers the "formation of 'a unitary European consciousness' [. . .] to be a premise indispensable to the constitution of a European federation of democratic states," the article "Federalist Tendencies"[59] specifies that a "widespread unitary European consciousness does not yet exist on our continent just as a widespread Italian consciousness did not exist during the Risorgimento. It was only the arms of Piedmont, Garibaldi, and the French that were able to bring about the 'miracle' of Italian unification. Attempts by Cavour and his successors to stoke popular movements that would have given at least a semblance of justification to the Piedmontese intervention were in vain. The plebiscites in the various elections were even less serious than the elections under the Fascist regime. And civil insurrections in the south over several decades showed what the people's real feelings were. Even then, a widespread Italian consciousness was not the basis — it was the consequence of unity. And nevertheless, the experience Italy gradually gained allowed the development of our political life in an ambiance of increasingly liberal and democratic institutions right up to the outbreak of the past war, when no one any longer thought of undoing it."[60]

The Roman federalist editors of *L'Unità Europea* in July-August 1943 thus understood the analogy of their action with the Risorgimento, almost as a continuation of Risorgimento teaching in another guise. "If a widespread European consciousness does not yet

---

international relations and values — an overhaul that would strongly deny the principle of absolute state sovereignty and reject territorial issues. [. . .] They posit this overhaul [. . .] so as to allow and ensure a general economic reorganization according to the principles of division of labor, the free transfer of productive forces and goods, and free access to sources of raw materials. [. . .] Is there any system other than a federal one that would allow and ensure this readjustment of economic life?"

[59] In the drafting of which, as I mentioned above, it is likely Eugenio participated, if only because — as the reader can ascertain in person — some of his observations, which we will now address, were already present in his letter to Altiero of May 1943. Notable also is the correspondence between Colorni's criticism of this conception of a European consciousness as "a premise indispensable to the constitution of a European federation" and the famous critique of preconditions for development that opens Albert Hirschman's *The Strategy* (1958).

[60] Am I wrong, or is there in this argument a reflection of the wisdom of "the teacher in fascist schools," gradually developed in dialogue with his students, that Eugenio showed so eloquently in his articles in 1937? (Colorni 2019, pp. 39–44).

exist," the article goes on, "what does exist in every country of the continent is Europeans, just as Italians existed during the Risorgimento in the different regions of the peninsula. And the task of these Europeans today is analogous to what those Italians managed to achieve at the time. They must give all their support to progressive forces in those countries able to take on the role of initiators of European federal unity — in opposition to the reactionary forces in their own country that support a patriotism that is narrow and exclusive. They must take care that unity does not become a cover for the hegemony of the winning countries; they must, through cooperation, institute a new order that truly ensures equal rights and opportunities for development for all peoples within the general frame of common interests."[61]

The section ends by pointing once again to historical relevance: "Either you argue that the United States of Europe must come into being 'spontaneously' through the free agreement of all the peoples of Europe, in which case you limit yourself to a long-term task of propaganda and education [. . .], or you maintain that the United States of Europe must rise in the period immediately after the war, essentially a work of the victorious powers — and in this case we must rapidly force the international situation in the direction we want, provoke interventions and support the ruling classes of whichever winning powers will give us the most trust, so that we can help them best achieve a federal program. We favor the second of these positions rather than the first, which we believe will create dangerous illusions and new disasters."

---

[61]"At the end of this war," the article concludes, "the situation that presents itself will be favorable as never before to European federal unity. But this situation will not last long. If we cannot make the most of it, if we let it go by waiting for the formation in all the countries of the continent of a European consciousness strong enough to express itself in the will of the majority of the population, we will give the old groups of sovereign states time to re-consolidate, and what follows will be the inevitable process of arms races, self-governing autarchies, and the politics of prestige and power until a new war breaks out. But wars are not exams that people can continually repeat until they reach the level of political education required to pass on to higher forms of organization. Another war would easily lead to European unification in the shape of imperialist domination by the country with the strongest military. And with that our civilization would be suffocated and without hope for an entire era."

13. This, then, is the general position behind Eugenio's new phase, launched in September-October 1943. He did not delude himself about what could be concretely accomplished. But he believed that only a militant commitment in the Nazi-Fascist war could give European partisans, peoples and countries a say in the possible genesis, right after the war, of a United States of Europe built by the victorious power or powers.

Thus, despite some previous concessions to the "contingent future" (counterbalanced by stressing the onerous tasks of the present), the political message of the second number of *L'Unità Europea* actually represents, as a whole, a re-proposition, in a more relaxed style suitable for the middle-brow reader, of the strategy Eugenio had already expressed in his letter to Altiero of May 1943.

It is true, on the other hand, that, since his arrival in Rome, Eugenio had worked hard (in the words of his letter to Altiero) "keeping an eye on developing events and trying to influence them using the most effective and unbiased methods." He reorganized and directed the Roman federalist microcosm (which on 26 and 28 July, among other things, printed and distributed at various points in the city two leaflets[62] containing an appeal for partisan struggle — the first of the Italian Resistance)[63]; he brought the newspaper into port;

---

[62]Solari Fund, Envelope 3, File 28. The photographed text of the two leaflets is in Tedesco 2014, p. 156. According to the testimony of Cerilo Spinelli (cit. in Rognoni Vercelli 1991, p. 86–87), "On 26 July Colorni, Usellini and I met to decide the position of the Federalist movement concerning the Badoglio proclamation. We immediately agreed that the idea that the war should continue alongside the Germans was absolutely unacceptable and that, instead, an appeal should be made to the Italian people to prepare for armed insurrection and partisan struggle. At this same meeting the three of us put together a manifesto expressing this position. We printed several thousand copies of this manifesto and distributed it widely in the universities and in several factories and even in the streets." "On 26 July," Leo Solari also recalled on the occasion of the 60th anniversary of Colorni's death (2004, p. 21), "the day after Mussolini's government was overthrown, Eugenio did not hesitate to issue a manifesto [. . .] circulated in thousands of copies, containing the first appeal in Italy calling for partisan struggle against the Germans. Only after 8 September, in fact, would other political forces pronounce themselves in Italy in favor of armed struggle."

[63]Of the two leaflets mentioned in the text, the second concludes with a nice "NAZIS OUT!" Unfortunately, on July 30 a group of distributors was intercepted by the army, so that Guglielmo Usellini and Cerilo Spinelli were arrested and "referred to the Military Tribunal" (Rognoni Vercelli 1991, p. 98, n. 5), while Eugenio luckily managed to slip away. Cf. also n. 36 in ibid. (p. 110) which states that Daniele Usellini, son of Guglielmo and Luisa Villani, "recalls that on 26 July 1943 working with Gigliola Spinelli, Luisa distributed this same

organized a group of young federalists predominantly of Jewish origin (which, however, failed to take root); and made contact with the socialist leadership.

Then on 18 August the Italian authorities finally allowed Altiero Spinelli to leave Ventotene. He arrived in Rome on the 19th and was occupied for a week with family gatherings and discussions with Eugenio, Ernesto (who had come down from Florence) and with other federalist leaders — precisely at the time when the PSI [Socialist Party] and the MUP were joining forces in the capital.[64] One of the questions in their discussions inevitably concerned eventually joining the PdA or the newly-formed PSIUP. As we know, Ernesto leaned toward the former and Eugenio the latter.[65] Altiero instead decided to remain independent.

With Eugenio and Ernesto, he then decided to organize the 27–28 August meeting in Milan, at the home of Rita and Mario Alberto Rollier,[66] "attended by Manlio Rossi-Doria, Franco Venturi, Vittorio

---

flyer by throwing it from a city trolly — the flyer that incited the armed struggle against the Nazi-Fascists and which cost Guglielmo and Cerilo Spinelli prison terms."

[64]This happened on 22 and 23 August at the home of Oreste Lizzadri. Following this, Pietro Nenni, finally freed from internment at Ponza, became secretary of the PSIUP and director of *Avanti!*, with Pertini and Andreoni as deputies. Colorni took part in one of the first executive meetings, supporting the federalist thesis so that in the program declaration of the PSIUP of August 25 (see *Avanti!* Of 26/8) among the objectives to be pursued (point 7) was "the launch of Europe towards a Federation of States, [as] the beginning of a Union of socialist republics." In a noted interview, Sonia Schmidt asked Altiero Spinelli: "The program of the PSIUP after 25 July 1943 contained a short passage in which the party calls for the creation of a free federation of states with the aim of destroying the capitalist structure of society in Europe etc. Can you tell me if this passage came from Colorni?" "The federalist passage in the PSIUP program [. . .]," Altiero replied, "came from Eugenio Colorni. It was his condition for [later] joining the leadership of the PSIUP." (Now in Spinelli 1985, p. 205–06).

[65]"Both Ernesto and Eugenio," Altiero later recalled (Spinelli 1987, p. 27–28), "pressed me during those days to join the action party or the socialist party. Both parties, they told me, were now engaged in the formation of their leading cadres and in seeking their programmatic identity; I would automatically be part of the leadership team [. . .] and together we would have significant influence in the development of their policy [. . .]. Eugenio introduced me to Nenni [. . .]. I spoke to him at length about the need to begin preparing now to think in terms not only of national democratic restoration, but also of building a European democratic power. Nenni listened, nodded and finally declared that he completely agreed with us. Leaving the visit Eugenio was jubilant [. . .]. I shook my head in disbelief. [. . .] Nenni would have taken twenty years to clear his mind [. . .] and ask me for help."

[66]Rita Isenburg Rollier had known Eugenio for some time, and both the Rolliers had met Ursula Hirschmann in 1938 at Forte dei Marmi. During Eugenio's imprisonment and exile,

Foa, and Leone Ginzburg, among others" — the meeting that (viewed in retrospect) saw "the birth of the European Federalist Movement."[67] Daniele Pasquinucci writes that on that same occasion "Colorni also played an important role in defining the strategy and organization of the association, and [. . .] successfully defended the idea that, as the 1941 *Manifesto* had said, the federalists should structure themselves not as a party but as a movement."[68]

"The reconstruction of the way the conference unfolded," wrote Cinzia Rognoni Vercelli, "is possible today thanks to a document that I think could be considered the minutes of the founding conference of the European Federalist Movement. [. . .] The handwritten notes [Mario] Rollier took during the conference have also been preserved."[69] Unfortunately, however, as I have personally verified,

---

"the Rolliers were Ursula's point of contact when she was in Milan." In addition, it was at the Rollier's, on 1 August 1943, that Ada Rossi again embraced her husband Ernesto after his release (Rognoni Vercelli 1991, p. 71 and p. 87–88).

[67]Bumbaca 2004, p. 47. At the end of the conference (attended by 31 people) the six *Political Theses* prepared by Altiero Spinelli were approved with some formal changes (see below), "which translated the guidelines contained in the Ventotene Manifesto into programmatic and organizational instructions." "The morning of the second day," reported Ada Rossi, "the participants were surprised and 'deluged' by an immense thunderstorm and arrived in via Poerio (the Rollier's) soaking wet. Mario (Rollier) got them undressed and wrapped in sheets while their clothes were hung in the sun, which had come back out 'after the storm.' The conference immediately resumed very earnestly and reconsidering it today I am moved and I have to laugh when I think of that meeting of men in 'Roman togas' setting out to build Europe" (Rognoni Vercelli 1991, p. 88–89).

[68]Pasquinucci 2010, p. 283–84. Unfortunately, the current narrative of the European Federalist Movement has always underestimated Colorni's contribution — in the dialogues with Altiero, the cultural background of the *Ventotene Manifesto*, the first continental leadership of the Federalist Movement, the preparation of the founding conference in Milan, the federalist (and socialist) role in the Resistance, and the editing of the final edition of the *Manifesto*. A disgraceful attitude, frankly, and one that has gone on for decades.

[69]Cf. Rognoni Vercelli, 1991, p. 89. Prof. Rognoni Vercelli in fact added (ibid. p. 99–100, n. 12) that along with Eugenio Colorni's letter to Ernesto Rossi of 5 August (cf. below) "which anticipates the themes that would later be the focus of the plenary discussions at the conference [. . .] Rita [Isenburg Rollier] found [in her basement, in a box of Mario's documents] some papers that seemed to be the minutes of some antifascist meeting. She showed them to me and, with some excitement, I recognized that here were the minutes of the founding conference of the MFE [European Federalist Movement]. Finally, after forty years of talking about the federalist conference, we had found the document that would serve as objective confirmation of the testimony of those who had been present at the time, but who with the passing of years, had given versions that were somewhat vague and sometimes divergent one from the other." "Stored at the Rollier residence in Milan," the professor went on (ibid. p. 89) "the document proved to consist of thirteen manuscript

both documents have now disappeared. And my repeated attempts
to located them with the help of assistants and friends of Professor
Rognoni Vercelli (who died prematurely in the meantime) all came
to nothing. Reliance on the professor's assessments and Edmon-
do Paolini's transcription[70] of the minutes is therefore unavoidable
(without being able to compare them, as I would have liked, with
the two original documents).

14. In any case, it is worthwhile scrolling quickly through Paolini's
transcription of the minutes in search of Eugenio's contributions.[71]

27 August Meeting
   Information on Current Situation [. . .]
   Proposals for Action [. . .]
   Deliberation on assignments: Quarti and Rollier will make
contact with the German army. Colorni and Spinelli will present
a bilingual manifesto for the Italian-German army. Don Gilardi,
Cristofoletti, Roberto Usellini, Rollier will make contact with senior army personnel. [. . .]
   1. Form of Organization of the Movement [. . .]
   2. Character of Our Promotion Campaign [. . .]
   Colorni: Definition of the position of those present concerning
the MFE. [Replies from Rossi, "This is a meeting of sympathizers,"
and Spinelli, "Do not make hasty decisions. For now we'll present
our working guidelines. There won't be any decisions today."]

---

pages written in three different hands whose identity was to me uncertain. Spinelli's hand-
writing was in any case obvious in some of the glosses in the margins. These were mainly
corrections, added in all probability after a re-reading of the minutes, concerning important
points in the discussion." Finally, Rognoni Vercelli added in a note (ibid, p. 100, n. 13)
that "there are 21 handwritten sheets by Rollier [. . .]. They are actual notes and are very
schematic. This document and the minutes are complementary and complete each other on
some points." The two documents (cf. ibid, p. 13) were part of the "Rollier fund, donated
by the family [. . .] to the Luciano Bolis European Foundation and filed with the Historical
Institute of the Faculty of Literature and Philosophy at the University of Pavia."
[70]Paolini 1996, p. 316–25.
[71]The meeting starts with Altiero's agenda (followed only in part), a list of questions and
desires (Paolini 1996, p. 315–16). The drift of the meeting (to some extent informative) is
to bring the participants up to date on numerous federalist problems already discussed at
length by the veterans of Ventotene and their friends.

Colorni: Our activity will not be carried out only in the parties, but also through an independent newspaper. [. . .][72]

Colorni: It is institutions and not the will of the people that create liberty. [. . .]

3. *Organizational Problems* [. . .]

Colorni: Asks that the federalist idea also be formally supported within the parties. The MFE must attract the greatest possible number of young people to the federalist idea. [. . .]

[Cavallera: Speaks of the experience of what the PdA was like and how he tried to orient it. In the PdA there were two tendencies — one that wanted action directed at the masses, and the other at the middle class. He tried to strengthen the one aimed at the masses, orienting it towards federalism. He found the prevailing currents in the PdA to be those of a party for the masses. Concerning the MFE, he saw it take root within the party. He asks the federalists not for ideological action, but for an energetic entry into the parties so as to merge them in a European orientation. Left to their own devices, the parties may move away from federalist ideas. To influence them, these must become part of the parties themselves. Rollier confirms this, recalling his own personal experience.]

[Referring to these remarks] Colorni: He finds himself in these same conditions in the Socialist Party.

4. *Whether or not to continue with the underground movement* [. . .]

28 August Meeting [. . .]

Colorni: Will our movement be cultural or political? If it were based only on the idea of the intellectuals, Rossi would be right [*passim*], but since the fall of Fascism we've been a political movement and our actions will be political. Our foundations cannot be strictly liberal-socialist. As regards the formation of a European consciousness, it is necessary to establish to what extent it is to be achieved; to create this sort of awareness, European institutions would have to be created. Our movement will spell out the ideolog-

---

[72]At this point the minutes continue as follows: "Spinelli: Presents and reads several federalist theses. Damiani: We need to develop relations with various movements — more explicitly, with the Communist Party. Colorni: Postpone this issue to a more appropriate moment."

ical points that will clarify the ideas of others as well. [. . .]

Colorni: [participates in the discussion on communism] Requests an amendment to article 4 [the political theses, in the end corrected].[73] He speaks about Russia.

Plan for Work in the PdA and the PS

[Responding to Rossi: We all have to take sides within the political parties. Where this proved impossible we would turn directly to the masses.] Colorni: Agrees. But the action of the parties must not compromise direct action. The parties must accept this explicitly. [. . .]

Colorni: The Rossi issue is closely related to that of Spinelli. If Rossi joins a party, then Spinelli does too. [. . .]

[Rossi wants to join the PdA to strengthen the left wing. Spinelli should join the PS. Ginzburg: Spinelli shouldn't always be considered the heretic — he has to take on leadership functions. Venturi: Spinelli shouldn't join the PS. Rollier: Spinelli shouldn't join the PS. He should join the PdA. Morpurgo: Spinelli in the left wing of the

---

[73]"Militarism, despotism and war can be eliminated by creating a European Federation to which those sovereign powers can be transferred that concern the common interests of all Europeans — those which today, in the hands of national states, are only instruments of ruin. Armaments, freedom of international commerce, currency, the determination of national frontiers, the administration of colonial territories not yet able to govern themselves, intervention against any attempts to revive totalitarian regimes — in short, the administration of peace and freedom throughout Europe must be the provenance of the executive, legislative and judiciary powers of the European Federation. In the sphere in which federal sovereignty applies, the inhabitants of the various states must possess European citizenship in addition their national citizenship — that is, they must have the right to choose and control federal governments and be subject directly to federal laws." (Spinelli 1984, p. 336–37 and Paolini 1996, p. 294.) This refers to point 4 of "Some theses" of August 3, 1943 (and therefore from Ventotene) "which with slight formal corrections," wrote Spinelli (1984, p. 335), "became the *Federalist Theses* adopted a few weeks later by the European Federalist Movement at the time of its foundation in Milan on August 27." What were these slight formal corrections? Unfortunately, we do not have the original minutes, nor Rollier's notes (which were apparently stolen) and not even the Ventotene draft of the Theses — so we cannot know. Because Paolini informs us (in n. 138, p. 310) that "The *Theses* [presumably in their definitive form] were printed in number 3, September 1943, of *Unità Europea* and, subsequently, in Spinelli" 1984. Now, the wording of point 4 of the text in Paolini 1996 is identical to Spinelli 1984, while on the contrary, the minutes of 27–28 August, transcribed by Paolini himself maintain, as mentioned, that Colorni had proposed an amendment to point 4, and that this request provoked the following discussion: "Foa — A solution that is federalist in appearance but actually conceals either Russian or English hegemony must certainly be excluded. Rossi — Exclude totalitarianism. Spinelli — Re-reads the point concerning the political theses. Rollier — reads the amendment to point 4. [Which one?] The definitive text is agreed." The one above.

PdA."] Colorni: Himself in the PS. Not Spinelli. [. . .]"

Colorni: Argues that there is much scope for action in the MUP. Spinelli should join it.[74]

Giussani and Colorni: Relations with the Communist Party.

International Relations [. . .]

Publication of Our Writings [. . .]

Colorni: Present our writings with a preface indicating that they are a position taken by a member of the MFE and not an ideological text. [. . .]

Financing [. . .]

Organization [. . .]

Colorni: The cultural work is entrusted to Rossi and Rollier in Milan. Spinelli and Colorni will take care of the newspaper in Rome. The newspaper will be weekly. [. . .]

Colorni: Rossi and Spinelli will make up the supreme tribunal for federalist issues. Advises organizing meetings of people new to federalist ideas — they should pay dues, distribute newspapers, etc; groups of 'friends of the newspaper,' weekly courses on federalist issues. [. . .]

Colorni: Establish contacts with elements of the various parties. Spinelli and Rossi appoint the committee: Torino: Venturi and Banfi [;] Milano: Giussani and Rollier [;] Roma: Colorni, [Luisa] Usellini and Ginzburg.

Position of Italians in Case of English Occupation [. . .]

Colorni: Regarding the newspaper, it remains our intention that its character will be illegal and combative. It will provide concrete slogans, not least against the government. The newspaper will consist of a basic article, an article with writings from Ventotene, an

---

[74]Clearly, at the Milan conference Colorni still considered the PS and MUP to be two distinct entities, but as mentioned (cf. n. 64), they had already begun their process of fusion, launching the PSIUP. At the end of the conference Eugenio returned to Rome (while Altiero, Ernesto and Ursula, with the children, traveled to Switzerland to follow and promote the birth of the Federalist Movement in other European countries). In Rome, Eugenio formally joined the PSIUP and asked that Altiero be enrolled as well. Colorni — Spinelli later wrote in his diary on 4–6 July 1948 (1989, p. 13) — "asked on his own initiative and unbeknownst to me that I be admitted into the Socialist Party, which was opposed by Pertini. When Colorni told me, I replied that I didn't appreciate at all what he had done, since I didn't want to join. [. . .] Colorni and Andreoni [PSIUP vice-secretary] asked me to join the Socialist Party and I refused."

article on Sicily,[75] and a fourth page with controversies and discussions between the federalist current and the other parties."

So what took place in that small federalist firmament with thirty-one participants was that, in addition to making a constructive contribution to the launch of the MFE, Eugenio sought to emphasize certain specifics that speak volumes about his intentions: a political movement aimed at constructing European institutions (which would also promote the gradual formation of a European consciousness); work within the parties, not ruling out direct intervention;[76] the opportunity represented by the MUP (see below) to develop mass initiatives from below; the need for a weekly federalist newspaper as a battle flag (which he was unable to achieve); the desire (frustrated) to involve Altiero in the Roman federalist and socialist sphere.[77]

* * *

Socialist Federalism

15. Let us take a step back. On the crest of the wave, at the high points of the struggle — as I mentioned above — especially regarding opportunities that are highly favorable intellectually and socially (like the one created in Rome following 25 July), the mind can take flight, we seem to glimpse the distant future — as if it were already in the cards, almost at hand. Then, when this powerful and Socratic "mirage" fails to materialize and we fall back to earth and find

---

[75]Following the liberation of the island that started with the allied landing at Gela on 10 July, a political-military precursor to 25 July (fall of Mussolini).

[76]This was wording that in a certain sense overturned what had been said in his letter to Rossi of 5 August (which will be discussed: cf. sec. 16 and n. 82 below) in which Eugenio entertains the possibility that direct action should be flanked by actions to be developed within the parties. Evidently, his earlier perplexity had been resolved in favor of this later eventuality.

[77]Another goal he was unable to achieve, but which indirectly clarifies his attitude toward his friend. Eugenio, personal vicissitudes aside, was linked to Altiero by relations of esteem, friendship, respect and consideration, above all for his abilities in working out ideas and political initiatives. At the same time, Colorni fought for his own ideas (which, as we have seen, did not necessarily correspond with those of Spinelli). On one hand, he had to let Altiero live and express himself freely, and on the other there was a need not to lose sight of him and to influence him — a duality, typical of Eugenio's theory of love, which, not surprisingly, we find in many of his activities.

ourselves faced with a sea of difficulties, we often put aside hopes and motivations and focus instead on the specific, material, urgent things that we want to achieve. And nevertheless, after a certain time, we feel the need to somehow find our feet again. . . .

All this happened to me (yet again, but in a flash!) skimming through "Movement or Party?" the third article in *L'Unità Europea* n. 2, when I came across this definition of federalism: "it is a conception of peoples' process of becoming, based on the assumption — now tragically borne out by facts — that the era of national states is over, that today we cannot speak of the internal order of nations, of progress, of social conquests etc., except in the context of an international order without which people and their communities become an instrument of imperialism. Federalism is therefore a need that can be felt, and is felt, by people of every party, class, nation, race or religion, and as such goes beyond the traditional schemes of political parties proper."

This is an argument which, applied to today's world, immediately struck me as both true and not true. "True" as a *trend* which is part of a medium- to long-term historical journey (which the events of the European Union itself are a part of) that is now benefiting from robust globalization. But also "not true" because we still have to reckon with national states whose numbers have in the meantime increased to a worldwide total of nearly two hundred.

Thus, nearly eight decades after these words were written, the human condition in which we find ourselves points to enlisting federalist means to encourage processes of freedom, fraternity, and equality aimed both at liberating and enhancing productive forces and at promoting cultural, technological, social, and civil progress, but all the while containing, opposing, and as far as possible, gradually "taming" the aggressive, nationalistic, and imperialist aspects of the nations of the world (small and large) — this is the challenge currently that torments us.

The perplexity aroused by the multifaceted and complex nature of the task was expressed even in the title of the article and needed to be resolved. And indeed, "Movement or Party?" goes on to argue that "what suits it [federalism] best in this, its sowing season, is to be called a political *movement* rather than a party, since the task thus falls to the parties themselves as a first and most urgent requirement, and the members can in due course belong to any party as long as its aims do not conflict with federalism's fundamental purpose. But to avoid any misunderstanding, it ought to be specified that calling it a *movement* suits federalism not so much because it limits itself to the task of building an internationalist consciousness (which is also among its aims), but in so far as it allows its members a certain breadth and variety of views towards social ideologies and government programs," which, I believe I can safely say, are more closely linked to the affairs of states and are therefore not so easily pushed in the direction of a federalist solution.

Moreover, shortly thereafter, on August 5, 1943, Eugenio Colorni wrote in an even more explicit (succinct and articulate) way to Ernesto Rossi (who, finally free, had asked him about the problem of whether or not to join the various parties, the Action Party in particular).[78] "From now on I don't think we should present ourselves just as a cultural movement aimed at spreading the federalist idea among its groups, but as a political organization offering well-defined ideas. The fall of fascism marked the beginning of an era in which European unity is no longer a distant ideal, but is present as a feasible possibility — and for this reason we have to be part of concrete daily political life, showing people how the words from the European unity guidelines are the clearest, most vibrant, and most immediately felt as responsive to the situation."

"This does not mean," Eugenio continues, "that we have to be a party — we do not in fact need to burden ourselves with a demanding program of internal, social, etc. policies, and we can tolerate divergent viewpoints concerning these problems; and also because the task we are proposing is not necessarily to take power, but essentially to act in such a way as to favor or bring about situations of international politics that take us in the direction of European unity. By now, our task should no longer have to be so much one of persuasion, but rather of real political action, making use of all the political

---

[78]This letter was found by Rita Isenburg Rollier among her husband's papers and shown to Cinzia Rognoni Vercelli: cf. above, n. 69. "The signature," the latter wrote (1991, p. 99, n. 12) "was illegible. But since the content led me to suppose that it could be a letter from Colorni, I showed it to Ursula, who confirmed my guess.

means available (promotion among the masses, action within the leadership of the parties, contacts with movements abroad, diplomacy, the use of "myths" and popular "magic words" etc.).[79]

Yes, of course, you might say — but did this mean operating within the parties or independently, turning "directly to the masses in our own name?" "A difficult problem to solve in the present state of affairs," replied Eugenio in this letter.[80] "To make things clearer," he continued, "we have to keep in mind that of the presently existing parties, from the PdA [Action Party] to the Communists, none has yet made direct contact with the masses, who have been effectively de-politicized by Fascism. For now, all the parties have a clientele composed of old pre-Fascist politicians and people who have been working underground. But the real masses, who for years and years have believed that democracy and socialism were tired relics of the past (the only conviction that Fascism was able to instill in everyone, even including the workers) — the real masses, how will they react to the actions of the various parties of today? Won't they be disheartened, even nauseated by the tired old phrases on offer? Won't they be much more ready to accept the word of European unity, as long as it is perceived concretely — that is, as addressing the present, urgent problem to be solved, without too many institutional and social trappings? I believe they will — and in the few experiences I've

---

[79]On the other hand, the article in *Unità Europea* had stated "A movement, not a party, because, given its revolutionary conception and its need to unify, [federalism] conducts its activities on a different level, not in opposition but parallel to what the various parties do, traditionally and structurally, when they pursue their struggle on national soil. Therefore the discipline that federalism imposes on its adherents is no less a commitment than it would be if it came from an actual party. Its character is therefore quintessentially political because, in keeping with its objective — otherwise vast and complex — it aims to mobilize any and all forces capable of working in its behalf, wherever they are found and under whatever progressive banner they serve. It aims to create its own organization, intent on spreading the federalist idea and remaining resolutely revolutionary in today's underground political life."

[80]In the meantime, at Ventotene, nervously awaiting his release, Altiero drafted the "Federalist theses," (which would be approved on 27–28 August in Milan) and wrote to Ernesto and Eugenio (on 6 August), "I think it would be advisable that whichever of you is in the Action Party should move with great energy. L'Empirico (Rossi) should immediately ask for full participation in the directorate. And Aldo (Colorni) should also not abandon the positions he can occupy in the socialist party. However, you must maintain your freedom of action, and commit yourselves to considering the discipline of the federalist movement superior to that of the parties. Anyone who does not intend to accept this would simply be considered a sympathizer."

had up to now in 'virgin' environments I felt an immediate response to what we had to say, much more alive and supportive than in the 'crafty' realm of politics. If this impression of mine should prove correct, then we ought to put our case directly to the masses, not using the various existing parties as intermediaries."

16. So the problem was not solved. It amounted to verifying this concrete fact on the ground — something that the federalist group in Rome was already doing; while at the same time keeping an eye on the chaotic and unexpected evolution of events, at a basic level as well as at the top.

In his "Letter to the Ventotene Federalists" of mid-July Eugenio had written (with bitter irony) that at the moment of his arrival in Rome the problem of a coup d'état had for several weeks been an immediate issue. "Senators, generals went to the king [. . .]. Various generals commanding army units spoke with representatives of the underground parties. They stated that they were ready to act if the masses took the initiative. The party representatives promised the support of the masses once the generals moved. So each was waiting for the other and everything stayed the way it was" up until 25 July, which marked the beginning of a phase that was fluid, uncertain, full of unknowns.

Evidently following the fall of Mussolini relations between the generals and underground movements intensified. But then, of course, Badoglio's police measures, September 8 and the Nazi occupation of Rome soon changed the cards on the table — not least for the Roman federalist group. Eugenio Colorni, who already in mid-July[81] had expressed the view that "we are at the point where we need to start to act," had in his heart evidently resolved the perplexity expressed in his letter of 5 August — he decided that the federalist movement would have to participate actively in the activity of the parties.[82]

---

[81]Cf. below, his "Letter to the Ventotene Federalists."

[82]Probably because in the worsening situation there was no longer room for a direct mass initiative on the part of the federalists (which, to spread and prosper required a political situation that was less heated). On the other hand, Eugenio had already written to Ernesto in his letter of 5 August that if "my impression [that they should appeal directly to the masses

Hence Eugenio's approach and subsequent accession to the PSIUP,[83] his brief "declaration of principles," — "The socialists and the European federation"[84] — and, finally, his attempt to intervene with the highest military and administrative circles of the country.[85] Indeed, faced with 8 September, Colorni immediately went to general Carboni and other senior officers to obtain weapons. On the 10th, he was at the wheel of a truck, distributing arms with Felice Dessy and Mario Zagari, when it was stormed by the population in

---

in their own name] proves wrong, then it would be better to act within the various parties – not so much by putting forward a federalist program as by pushing them a little at a time to take positions and direct their politics in a way that we think will serve the purposes of European unity. Therefore," he concluded, "we should move toward assuming leadership posts, and not only in the Action Party, but also — at least — in the Socialist Party, since with the Communist Party we have no chance." But even here, Eugenio's initial ideas of what to do within the parties would be quickly "registered" and modified by the lessons of current events — in the sense that federalist pressure on the socialist leadership that he would maintain over time would be vigorously supported and validated by the rapid penetration of federalist ideas at the base of the party — above all in the youth sector.

[83]"Especially after July 25, with the fall of the regime, [Colorni] resumed his contacts with comrades who had returned from confinement or left prison, establishing new ones or stitching up those interrupted by their sentencing. The work of reorganizing political activity intensified and led Colorni to devote himself to the organization of the PSIUP" (Bumbaca 2004, p. 46–47).

[84]This declaration, see below, was reported in its entirety by *L'Avvenire dei Lavoratori* 4 (25 Feb. 1944) (as part of the review article "Socialists for the United States of Europe": cf. Merli S. ed. 1992) and was published, after Eugenio's death, by *Unità Europea* n. 6 under the title "The socialists and the European federation. Eugenio Colorni's declaration of principles." According to Leo Solari (1980, p. 143), it soon became "the political platform of the federalist socialists"; but it is a bit convoluted — I think deliberately. In fact, reading it in parallel with *Unità Europea* n. 2 leads to the conclusion that it is an attempt (especially successful in form) to tune in to old ways of thinking so as to be able to "launch" new ideas almost surreptitiously, in summary form. (This is a "possibilist" procedure, which would be refined and developed by Albert Hirschman — starting with *Journeys* 1963.) As we will now see, Eugenio used this "declaration of principles" to build a socialist federalist trend, especially among young people.

[85]Following a script that he had inaugurated at Ventotene (Meldolesi 2015). In particular, during the Resistance, Eugenio maintained contact with the police chief, Guida, to the extent that he asked on his deathbed that Guida be informed. As Giuliano Vassalli wrote to Sandro Gerbi on 13 November 1995 (Solari Fund, Envelope 1, File 21) "To me it seems entirely plausible because these police officers of the fascist period often tried to make contact with their old prisoners and possibly help them. It also seems plausible to me that when Colorni was wounded, he asked that Dr. Guida at Police Headquarters be informed." In other words, there was a gray area inside the police-administrative hierarchy where, whether off their own bat or because of the way the war was going, people were preparing to . . . switch sides (Meldolesi 2019, Appendix).

the neighborhood of Montecitorio.[86] But the appeal for insurrection was not followed. At this point Eugenio began moving in the circles of the young socialists and was immediately given military responsibility in the underground PSIUP. Working with a group of socialist railway workers,[87] in late October Colorni became military leader in the northeast area of the city — from Flaminio to Pietralata and Settecamini. And from mid-November on he was the military officer for parts of the southern zone — Quadraro, Torpignattara, Centocelle, Quarticciolo, Giordani, and Pigneto.[88]

As he later recalled in his "Letter to the Ventotene federalists": "On 9 September I found myself, with only Breitarme [Braccialarghe] and Eustachio [Gigliola Spinelli], having to mobilize our forces for action. I put together a small team composed of about twenty people (the young people from the meetings that you [probably Guglielmo Usellini] attended as well), which functioned fairly well over those two days, doing what little it was possible to do. This team was associated with the PS, which I had joined as soon as I came back from Milan. In the following weeks it was clear to everyone that the problem of the teams was the most urgent, with the prospect of the British arriving in only a few days, and since my team, composed largely of Jews, had in the meantime broken up, and also because work with the teams required a serious level of organization, I decided to spend my time working with the teams in the PS. I was assigned a zone, which I still have [November 1943],

---

[86]Paolo Monelli, *Roma 1943*, Roma: Tipografia del Senato, 1945.

[87]From which arose the "National Group of Socialist Railwaymen" — according to *Avanti!* n. 10 (underground Roman edition of 30 Dec. 1943). "Eugenio," explained Antonio Tedesco, "was working with the group of action teams of the socialist railroad workers, a large organization inspired by the socialist railwayman Alessandro Sideri, [. . .] with the primary task of sabotaging German military transport. The railroad workers' organization stemmed from an initiative of Eugenio Colorni and Enrico Di Pietro. It brought together a hundred elements divided into nine groups that operated at different stations around the city."

[88]Undated testimony of a communist exponent of ANPI in memory of Eugenio Colorni: Solari Fund, Envelope 1, File 13. Referring to the military setup of the three parties on the left (PdA, PS and PSIUP), Eugenio himself wondered in his "Letter to the Ventotene Federalists," "How are these teams used? For the time being, only actions against the fascists are advisable and only these are carried out (especially against fascist spies). Actions against the Germans are allowed only when they leave no trace, because otherwise there would be reprisals that were too serious. What we mainly aim for are acts of sabotage. Many of these are planned and prepared; few are carried out."

and Eustachio and I applied ourselves to various relevant initiatives. I was so involved in this work that I had no opportunity to engage with politics."[89] For Eugenio it was thus a truly unexpected, stressful and tumultuous political and military transformation.

17. Nine months passed between the federalist meeting in Milan and Eugenio's death — an extremely intense but not much studied period of his life. The best approach in dealing with it is to get an overall idea, as convincing as possible, of what he was trying to do, and then follow step by step the development of some of the many covert activities that he set in motion.

The fusion, in retrospect highly improbable (but obviously possible!), of the intellectual with the man of action (or more precisely "in favor of action"[90]) — is the most striking characteristic in the testimony of those closest to Eugenio at the time. An accurate perception of the nature of Colorni's political life in Rome is impossible, according to Leo Solari, "without an effort to see the way his journey also reflects the spirit in which he dealt with other things as well and, more generally, with life — a spirit constantly affected by strong moral tensions, which thus held him to a rigorous stan-

---

[89]And of course there was no way he could go on with his intellectual work (in the natural sciences, philosophy, psychology, literary criticism). And yet, even at the height of his conspiratorial activities, Eugenio continued to think about it — this comes out clearly in the testimony of various witnesses and emerges vividly in his dialogues with young people and in the party school: cf. below. Nevertheless, what *Avanti!* published in memoriam on June 5–6 was undoubtedly true: "Once Rome was occupied [Colorni] threw himself into the organization of the Resistance, dodging management positions for that of the basic militant who leads the hard life of the conspiracy." But this was only a first step.

[90]"A passionate fighter," "a shining hero," Leo Solari called Eugenio Colorni in his commemoration of 24 March 1954. "He was not 'a man of action.' He was for action," he added perceptively in his commemoration of 6 May 1979 (Solari Fund, Envelope 1, File 4). "He was a man with a pure heart," wrote Sandro Pertini in 1978 (now in Colorni 1998, p. 173–74). "One night during the underground struggle he confessed to me that for him the problem of physical fear was very acute, which did not prevent him from doing his duty to the utmost. One day on the Colle Oppio I delivered a package of dynamite to him, I told him what it was and what the risks were. It was perfectly clear that Colorni was afraid. He took the package without hesitation and went on his way. I watched him and realized that with every step he was fighting and overcoming his fear. If there ever was a gold medal of the Resistance earned the hard way, it is his." This is an episode — the anonymous Communist partisan (cited above in n. 88) however observed — that shows the high level of danger that some of the top Psiup leaders were exposed to.

dard; a spirit that was reflective, problematical, investigative and introspective, and at the same time directed toward a coherent personal commitment to action; an anti-dogmatic spirit, iconoclastic and anti-conformist in every way, but not from a proud desire to be contradictory so much as out of a love of truth, an urgent need to *get to the bottom* of everything, to explore new pathways 'in search of the new'; a spirit irreducibly devoted to the idea of freedom not only because it is necessarily driven by a conceptual construction but, above all, out of a natural inclination to respect the way others feel and think."[91]

At the same time, it is worth listening to the fresh and poignant testimony, from June 1944, of Luisa Villani Usellini, Eugenio's partner. "There came a day when Eugenio Colorni put aside his already famous name. It was the day when he sprang into action — the 'day of courage' as he himself called it. Free of all ties to the past, ready for whatever the torrid time that was about to begin would bring, he became Angelo and appeared among us. So simple, so spontaneous and total was this gesture of his that many of us didn't know until the last who this man was, radiating strength and goodwill, who 'captured' us so instantly and almost magically, and without imposing himself or taking command, dragged us along in his wake and toward his idea.

He went into action after September 8, committing himself to the task of military organization in the different zones. In one rendezvous after the other he made contact with all those who felt the struggle was a necessity. Even in organizational work, he found a way to initiate people into political life, helping them clarify their ideas and put them in order. Without any premeditated plan, young people who wanted to contribute to the resumption of Italian po-

---

[91]Leo Solari 1985, p. 22. The interpretive problem before us — which will become clearer in the pages that follow — concerns the direct, credible witnesses we must depend on in our reconstruction. Each of them, in fact, in his or her own characteristics (personal, cultural, social, political), tends to comment on (and emphasize) one aspect or the other of the question. I therefore felt that to try and achieve some understanding (and thus render an idea of the way things actually were) I would do well to "stitch together" parts of these accounts, which were often quite different from one another. In this way I felt that in spite of some unevenness, it would be possible to hold the reader's attention regarding an undoubtedly multifaceted theme, because it basically concerns Eugenio's Promethean versatility.

litical activity both through practical action and intellectual energy tended more and more to gravitate towards him. The natural consequence was that these individual interviews turned into actual lessons, which Angelo organized with some of his better-prepared comrades, and which he firmly wanted to continue — until the rush of events forced everyone to more immediate duties."[92]

The ex-MUP Youth

18. So starting in September 1943 Colorni began moving regularly in the circles of the young socialists.[93] Concerning the Movement for Proletarian Unity (MUP), which most of these youths came from, he had initially given an opinion that was anything but favorable. "The MUP," he had written in his "Letter to the Ventotene Federalists," holds to the position of typical Marxist classist tradition. On the complete break between proletariat and bourgeoisie, absolute intransigence; they consider the PdA to be fascism in disguise [and] they reject any idea of a single front. . . ." In effect, in Eugenio's view, the group was ideological, sectarian. "In general, [they think] there is nothing essentially new to discover — that the terms of the struggle are still the traditional ones."

But the story didn't end there. "A party like this," he had gone on to say, "if it can wean the masses from the narcotics fed them by the communists, may serve a notable function in its explicit refusal to accept a static situation, acting as an agitator in a state of affairs that [otherwise] threatens to congeal into "there is nothing to be done." [. . .]

---

[92]"This well-trained group of young people," Luisa continued, "laid the basis of our Youth Federation, and Angelo, who had become editor of *Avanti!* continued to be their spiritual and political guide." Recollection of Luisa Villani Usellini written for *La rivoluzione socialista,* newspaper of the Socialist Youth Federation, which Colorni had contributed to re-establishing.

[93]Although not as a result neglecting his interest in the young communists. In his "Letter to the Ventotene Federalists," in mid-July (cf. below), he had in fact written of some of the members of the group of official communists, that they were "very well educated young intellectuals, some of whom are of the first rank, who without any experience or political preparation entered the party out of activist enthusiasm, considering this the party where there is the most to do (work among the masses, strikes, etc.). For now they are enthusiastic and extremely disciplined, but they make no mystery of their theoretical reservations (one of them spoke freely to me of the future task of intellectuals to combat "ignorance of Marxism") and do not rule out leaving the party the day they are no longer satisfied with it."

"With us, however, they would like to collaborate; indeed we have set up negotiations which, if they go well, may offer us an easy way to print our material [including, probably, the second issue of *L'Unità Europea*]. The basic idea here is that we will collaborate with *anybody* if there is mutual benefit favoring the underground work. This is essential if we want to accomplish anything; and we would ask that you do the same, eliminating personal friction as much as possible."[94]

On the other hand, the dramatic developments in the situation and the intense association he had begun with a group of these young people led his ideas to evolve (and also made him aware of the potential for conspiracy with ex-MUP members). As I have mentioned, it was this daily reconsideration of the situation, the way he was able to perceive it and assess it as it unfolded, that led Eugenio continually to alter his evaluations and behavior so that he was always ready, from one day to the next, to confront events. In this way Colorni put into practice as never before the main idea behind his philosophical reasoning, which was that thinking, in order truly to reflect an evolving present, must be ductile, flexible, open to continuous research and creative application, fearlessly reconsidering this or that aspect of reality.

It was true, in fact, that many even well-educated young people, intolerant of the temporizing of the traditional parties represented in the CLN [National Liberation Committee], were now oriented in favor of actively challenging the old managers.[95] "The Proletarian unity movement itself," Solari reported,[96] "arose from a concentration of groups with socialist leanings that had formed in 1939 in Rome, Milan and Venice [. . .] — it was mainly a youth group. During the

---

[94]"Therefore," Eugenio added, "in spite of your prohibition, we will send you their answer to their comrades there; indeed, we request [. . .] that you put yourselves at their complete disposal concerning the contacts they may need. You absolutely must do this — they have done us so many favors up to now (for example, they have greatly facilitated my stay here) that it would be downright ugly to refuse them this small service."

[95]A challenge effectively represented by the Proletarian Unity Movement and similar youth groups, such as "a student group that sprang up spontaneously at the University of Rome," the Revolutionary Association of Italian Students [ARSI], an organization "whose aim was to group together all the students 'of the left' and which had promoted the underground publication, starting in October 1943, of a student newspaper entitled *La nostra lotta* [Our Struggle]" (Solari 1964, p. 35).

[96]Solari 1964, p. 33–34.

war it had grown to a notable size, acquiring followers mainly among the younger generations, and penetrating deeply even among young reserve officers then under arms, including elements at the front or in war zones."

"The character of the MUP," explained Ruggero Zangrandi astutely in his authoritative *Il lungo viaggio attraverso il fascismo* [The long journey through fascism][97] "was twofold — on the one hand, right from the beginning it made contact with qualified anti-fascist elements who were already known and were some years older, though always with socialist leanings [. . .], and on the other, *it was able to impose itself* on these elements, who were more or less directly related to the PSI, and to claim an autonomous function of its own, both in representing the new generations that actually came from the fascist experience, and in pressing for unity, aiming to overcome the traditional and by now 'old' divisions between the socialist and workers' parties. Even without reaching a national level, the group became, especially in '41 and '42, a vast movement capable of interpreting the aspirations of the not insignificant numbers of young people of the time who were already completely detached from fascism but did not find feel at home among liberal-socialist groups, nor among the communists."

19. After 8 September and the Nazi-Fascist occupation of the capital, Eugenio joined the process of fusing together (as equals) the MUP and the PSI (which, as mentioned, gave rise to the Socialist party of proletarian unity — the PSIUP),[98] and found himself with a leading role within the new party.

---

[97]Zangrandi 1963, appendix 36 (cit. in Solari 1964, p. 33–34, n. 1). Italics mine.

[98]A trace of the fusion of the two parties thus remained even in the new party's name. Furthermore, "half the leadership posts were assigned to members of the MUP. This relationship was substantially preserved even when, following the arrival in Italy of Pietro Nenni, the leadership was reorganized" (Solari 1964, p. 34). "The phenomenon of an anti-fascist youth ferment, especially in the final phase of the dictatorship," wrote Zangrandi (1963, appendix 36; cit, in Solari 1964, p. 11 and 12) "is still one of the least explored areas of contemporary historiography." Within this turmoil, the socialist aspect "constitutes a unique case of a youth movement that arose spontaneously and autonomously within the country *becoming part of a traditional party,* bringing it its own stamp and particular characteristics."

"This is when Eugenio gives himself the name Angelo [. . .].
And it is in Rome that Eugenio [. . .] establishes a close relationship
with a political group that within the PSIUP had formed an embryonic opposition to the party leadership. The members of this group
(which had given itself the name 'political committee') were mainly
from the MUP [. . .]. The reservations it then expressed regarding
party leadership policy were focused on [. . .] institutional issues
[the monarchy first and foremost]. In reality the most important
reason for dissent was something else — something that had remained unspoken, but would increasingly make itself felt — a sub-
stantial difference in views regarding the role and the very existence
of the Socialist Party. In fact, this difference [. . .] would become the
predominant reason for disagreements with the majority of the PS-
IUP leadership, whose prevailing tendency was toward ever closer
relations with the Communists."[99]

In any case, if we want to understand the start of Colorni's
activities with the young socialists, a witness of great value in my
opinion is Claudio Pavone, who exited the scene due to a chance
error,[100] while his close friend Giuseppe Lopresti, military officer in

---

[99]Solari 2004, p. 21. The members of the "political committee" included Mario Andreoni
(deputy secretary of the PSIUP), Mario Zagari, the brothers Tullio and Alberto Vecchietti,
Achille Corona, Giovanni Barbera and Leo Solari. "Eugenio's pro-European perspective,"
Solari maintained "could not fail to take root in the orientation of that group," not least
because the penetration of federalist ideas among the young socialists was quick — as the
ARSI newspaper *Our Struggle* testified in December 1943 (see, above, n. 95), declaring,
"European unity will be our only salvation. [. . .] What the inertia of the masses, the skepti-
cism of politicians, the interests of capitalism, and the privileges of the ruling classes have
prevented from taking place, can now be accomplished" (cited in Solari 1964, p. 54, n. 2).
[100]A ridiculous episode, bordering on the grotesque. In *La mia Resistenza, Memorie di
una giovinezza* [My Resistance, Memories of Youth] (2015, p. 31–32) Pavone wrote, "On
22 October [1943], having nothing in particular to do, I walked for some distance around
the city and when evening came I had to go home [. . .]. I had a long way to walk and it
was almost curfew time. I was carrying a black, lawyers briefcase that had belonged to my
father and that I thought made me look respectable, and in it were some copies of *Avanti!*,
some socialist leaflets and mimeographed forms for organizing armed bands [. . .]. At the
start of via Cagliari a big car with the window down was parked in front of a main building
entrance that looked shut. To me it seemed like a great opportunity to throw in some of
the publicity leaflets I was carrying, which I did; then I crossed the street and headed for
via Alessandria. Right away I heard footsteps running behind me. 'Maybe they're not after
me,' I thought, perhaps to exorcise the danger, 'I shouldn't start running.' But I didn't even
have time to turn into via Alessandria before two arms had grabbed me on each side and
two plainclothes agents wordlessly led me back to the black car."

the area, continued to work alongside Eugenio up until Lopresti's capture (prelude, unfortunately to his martyrdom).[101]

In the obituary "Homage to Lopresti," Claudio Pavone recalled, written shortly before Eugenio himself was killed by the Fascists (and published after his death: cf. below), "Colorni wrote in emotional tones that the meeting with Lopresti had completely removed the reticence, not to say mistrust that had surfaced among the older generation. Even young people born and raised under Fascism — this was his observation — could come to anti-fascism through their own difficult paths, which were not always imaginable by anti-fascists with their older form of political militancy. [. . .] I knew Eugenio Colorni for hardly more than a month," he added,[102] "an intense and exceptional month between the end of September and the end of October 1943, when I was arrested. I met him with my friend Giuseppe Lopresti, who was only a little older than me but much more advanced culturally and politically. [. . .] Immediately after 8 September, in the grip of the suffering we felt at seeing the inglorious disintegration of the country's civil and military structures, we joined the Italian Socialist Party for Proletarian Unity. We wanted to get involved, and this was the party that seemed most likely to satisfy our desire for action and at the same time allow us to achieve a level of maturity that we felt we had not yet reached. Being posted as assistants alongside Eugenio Colorni, head of the Appio-Esquilino-Prenestino military sector, was a lucky circumstance for us. [. . .] Lopresti and I had had a Catholic upbringing

---

[101]Lopresti, as Giuliano Vassalli recalled (2004, p. 39), became "area commander; he was a hero. I remember that when he was taken, and it was not only him but a notable group of socialists, in February [1944], everyone was naturally afraid for what might be revealed. I remember Pepppino Graceva, our commander, saying [. .], 'no no, there's nothing to fear from Lopresti — his Catholic upbringing was so strict [. . .] his behavior will surely be heroic,' — and it was, right up to when he was shot at the Fosse Ardeatine."

[102]Pavone 2004, p. 33–34. Nevertheless, clearly the memory of his influence remained alive and moving in Pavone's mind. "The meeting with Colorni," Pavone explained (Ibid. p. 33), came to constitute an episode in what Marc Bloch called the creation of a long generation. This is a generation created not on the basis of data but of a common and intense experience at a crucial moment in life, whatever one's date of birth. Colorni was barely ten years older than we were, but for us he represented those who, whether convicts, internees, or exiles, had always opposed fascism and now offered their hand. His moral authority was immense."

and we were laboriously emerging from it. [. . .] Our attraction for
socialism came from our desire to escape from fascism not by backing out the entrance, but by taking the exit, which we first needed
to find. The Communist Party seemed, from this point of view, too
frozen to fully satisfy this need we still had to search and inves-
tigate. [. . .] Colorni [. . .] spoke to us early on about his study of
Leibniz. We were immediately impressed by the great willingness
he showed to talk to two young people, outspoken and resolute but
also a little lost, about both the needs of the underground organization and the deepest problems of humanity. The Resistance was one
of those times when a precious connection like this can take place.
Colorni made us feel it was possible by revealing among us a clear
elective affinity."

Pavone (who later became known as a great archivist and a distinguished historian of the Resistance) went on to write:[103]

> For us Colorni was the ideal leader and teacher. [. . .] It might seem
> strange that at the same time that he was distributing underground
> newspapers and preparing an insurrection, he was also debating
> weighty problems that have burdened humanity for centuries. But
> in fact this was one of the uplifting characteristics of that situation,
> and the fascination Colorni held for two young people like Lopres-
> ti and me came precisely from our seeing him as the symbol of that
> fusion. His attitude towards us was affectionate and open, and we
> could speak to him about any problem that concerned us. He was
> barely ten years older, but in our eyes he held the fascination of an
> old anti-fascist militant who had known prison and internment
> and had the intellectual prestige of someone who came from a cul-
> tural education different from ours.

20. This work with young people moved forward with great energy in those months and was extraordinarily important for Eugenio;

---

[103]Pavone 2010, p. 206. He wrote, among others, a text that has now become a classic: *Una
guerra civile. Saggio storico sulla mortalità nella Resistenza,* Torino 1991. [*A Civil War:
A History of the Italian Resistance* (2013). Stanislao Pugliese (ed.). Eng tr. by Peter Levy,
David Broder. London: Verso Books]. For our purposes, cf. especially Chap. 8.

not least because many of the successful actions were in fact led by the young socialists.[104]

But at a certain point the moment arrived when even "Angelo" had to scale down his commitment to area work and action-team building. He said as much in his "Letter to federalist friends in Switzerland" in November 1943, which marked the passage from an almost exclusive concentration on the military side of the Resistance to a renewal of his interest in federalist politics. The letter was a short "report," an important document divided into four parts: *The political-military situation, Military action by the political parties, Political positions of the various parties, Federalist movement.*[105]

In the first place, Eugenio's assessment of the political and military situation in Rome is without doubt of great interest. "There are not a great many Germans in Rome, and so far they haven't carried out excessive acts of terror, apart from the deportation of the Jews, which was truly brutal.[106] Evidently they are afraid of the Vatican and the various foreign embassies. They constantly circulate the rumor that all healthy men will be picked up, urging them to come forward voluntarily, but hardly anyone does. The city is full of people who live in a state of illegality (officers who failed to report, wanted politicians, men who have escaped from work service, etc.), but they circulate undisturbed and are not stopped in the street.

---

[104]"Nuclei of young socialists," reported Leo Solari (1964. p. 36–37), "were always present in the various actions and demonstrations organized jointly by young anti-fascists of various political leanings, demonstrations held repeatedly at the University of Rome (until they forced its closing). The young socialists [. . .] had [. . .] been actively present in organizing the "Gaps." [Patriotic Action Groups] Among other things, a Gap of the ARSI (cf. above, n. 95), whose members included the young socialists Louchard and Congedo, had penetrated the Batteria Nomentana barracks and brought away arms and munitions. Another Gap composed entirely of young socialists had raided the Forte di Pietralata, eliminating the sentinels and seizing notable quantities of arms. Groups of young socialists organized by Solari in collaboration with ex-officers of the army had [. . .] carried out various actions."

[105]It is no coincidence that, publishing it for the first time, Solari placed it as the reference point of his 1964 book on the Socialist Youth Federation (cf. in this regard, the notes on pp. 43 and 48). What these hurriedly written pages "cannot express," reads the title page of the volume, "and what remains of the political or moral significance of the action of the youth of the 'Socialist Revolution' is dedicated forever to the memory of one who for young socialists of the 'Resistance' was a guide in the struggle, a teacher and friend — Eugenio Colorni."

[106]Eugenio refers here to the tragic 16 October, when the German SS and the Fascist police rounded up a thousand Roman Jews, who were then deported to Auschwitz.

The police have come looking for people at their homes[107] [. . .] but almost reluctantly, without pressure or excessive searching.

Telephones are not tapped, even though everybody says they are. The Ovra [Fascist secret police] is not operating. On the other hand, there are numerous Fascist informers and many Gestapo agents who are operating, but they carry out their searches in Badoglio's military circles rather than in ours. Nevertheless, many arrests have been made in our ranks as well[108] [. . .]. The police, the PAI [Italian African Police], the Fascists and the Germans operate with a certain amount of independence from one another. Nevertheless, all the authorities are totally compliant with the Germans, who give them whatever they ask for; and there are truly scandalous cases of criminal cowardice."[109]

"The result of all this," Eugenio added further on, "is that the political parties are able to act with a certain facility, in spite of the difficulties and dangers. There is in any case vastly more political life than there was under Fascism, even very recently. And there is a combative atmosphere that leads people to confront the dangers with relative cheerfulness. The underground papers are buzzing, the streets are full of anti-German and anti-Fascist graffiti that the police are unable to erase completely, and each of us has a constant sense of solidarity from the entire population." This was without doubt an unexpected and encouraging conclusion.

Taking Control of the Situation

21. So how shall we judge this brief picture of the Roman situation of the time? If we compare this opening with that of the "Letter to the Ventotene Federalists" of four months earlier it is clear that the situation has changed. But its author has a different edge as

---

[107]Twice for Altiero and once for Cerilo Spinelli.

[108]Which included Sandro Pertini, Giuseppe Saragat, "and several others with them, but no excessively serious charges were filed."

[109]"The fascists," Eugenio continued in this letter, "are utterly miserable. Most of them are school children 16–18 years old, and they lack the courage even to mount provocations. Even the Germans despise them. They had announced big demonstrations for October 28th [anniversary of the March on Rome], and our teams were all set to react. But at the last moment, by order of the Germans, they didn't show up, so throughout the day we didn't see a single fascist in the streets."

well. He has been through an intense period of organizational and military work which has given him confidence in his abilities, both conspiratorial and political. Even though disguised, and despite enormous difficulties, the "Letter to Federalist Friends in Switzerland" brims with enthusiasm. It is an analytically thorough, crystalline letter, full of details that make it clear that Eugenio has found the "guiding thread" of his work; and it displays, within the limits of the possible, a certain mastery of the situation. He seems to want to convince his far-off friends that it is in Rome that the future will be decided, and that the game is really on.[110]

What is perhaps most striking is that the daily concrete monitoring of his own work constantly pushed Eugenio to better articulate and reformulate his point of view (almost as if he had theoretical and practical feelers that would allow him to adapt continuously, and with a grain of salt, to the sometimes unpredictable and harsh evolution of the real situation). A comparison of this letter with the beginning of the one he wrote to Altiero in May 1943 makes it clear that Eugenio now believed he had successfully overcome some of the situation's implicit dangers (probably including analytical and ideological inertia), and had therefore managed to ... "engage."

Turning to the text, the second section deals with *Military action by the political parties*. "Throughout the Badoglio period" [25 July to 8 September], Eugenio argued, "the political parties were unable to get anything from the military. They therefore found themselves totally unarmed at the moment of the armistice and, still worse, without organized teams that would have allowed them to participate in the struggle. All the same, some things were done, albeit chaotically and with no luck. Amid the total disintegration of the army there was a feeling that the message of the anti-fascist movements had a strong grip on the masses; and mainly we saw what should have been done but hadn't. From 8 September on, we began working feverishly to avoid ending up in the same state of impotence when the next clampdown came; the first thing was the organization of the teams."

Clearly, here Eugenio saw his organizational and military work

---

[110]Cf., in this regard, the judgment at the beginning of the letter that we mentioned above in n. 21.

of the last two months and more with the socialists as part of a healthy process of understanding and transformation of the present state of affairs that had involved the whole of Roman anti-fascism. "This task," he continued, "has occupied all the organizational activity of the three parties on the left (PdA, PSI, and PCI), who have joined together in a "leftist bloc" in the Liberation Committee. What the prospects might be of this effort succeeding, even I — though I'm in it up to my neck — can hardly say. Certainly there has been notable progress right from the start. Many teams have been put together, the tripartite commands (that is, of the parties together) work well both downtown and in the suburbs; we can mobilize the teams quite rapidly; some actions have already been carried out. But the most serious obstacle, one the whole organization has to deal with, is the lack of weapons."[111]

In addition, this military organization had been put together in anticipation of the coming "squeeze" represented, first and foremost, by the (mistakenly) expected arrival of "the British." In fact, Colorni went on, in "preparation for an eventual state of emergency the city has been divided into eight zones, and these into sectors. The operating unit is a nucleus composed of three teams of 5 men each. A team has to stay together or be able to assemble quickly during an emergency under the zone command, jointly held by three commanders from the three parties, who will live in the same house. The actions to be carried out will be responses to possible looting, assaults on arms stores or food stores, possible actions of harassment against German rearguards (apart from retreating troops moving through the city), and above all, during the interval between the departure of the Germans and the arrival of the English, the occupation of strategic points and important buildings, and the maintenance of public order, so that when they arrive they will find the city in the hands of party forces."[112]

---

[111]"I think," Colorni added, "the three parties will be able to gather perhaps about two thousand men in the teams; but less than half of these are armed, and badly. For the anonymous Communist partisan (cited above, n. 84) of the ANPI, perhaps a quarter of the total were Socialists, supported by another 700 militants.

[112]"There is a central tripartite command," Eugenio adds, composed of Riccardo Bauer for the PdA, Giorgio Amendola for the PC, and Sandro Pertini for the PS, replaced after his arrest by

22. So at the time, in November 1943, this was the way Colorni and many other anti-fascists imagined the liberation of Rome would actually come about.

The question that remains is what might be (or ought to be) the role of politics in all this? In the following section, concerning the *Political Positions of the Various Parties*, Eugenio's brief "report" to distant friends spoke directly to this issue as it stood at the time.

"The Liberation Committee is composed of 6 members." Casati for the Liberals, Bonomi (and Ruini) for the Labor Democrats, De Gasperi for the Christian Democrats, La Malfa for the Action Party, Nenni for the Socialist Party, and Scoccimarro for the Communist Party. Its activity, Colorni realistically pointed out, "consists of nothing more than a continual tug of war between the three parties on the right and those on the left concerning anti-monarchic and republican prejudices. [. . .] What weakens the left in this action is the attitude of the communists, who are extremely accommodating, and the other two parties' [PdA and PSI] fear that they will be isolated in the Liberation Committee. Nobody has the courage to take responsibility for such a break; so we move forward with this behind-the-scenes disagreement that will come to the fore the moment the English arrive."

"What will happen then?" Eugenio asks, finally coming to the point. He answers that "there are two scenarios. 1) The parties on the left will successfully present a situation in the city in which they are the arbiters, completely undermining the authority of Badoglio and the king in the eyes of the English so as to get them removed (I am told that Badoglio has had little success so far in attempting to put together an army); in which case all six parties will come to power in a sort of six-person 'Public Safety Committee' [. . .]. 2) Alternatively, the English will leave the power with the monarchy, probably with a regency, in which case the three parties on the right will surely come to power; and what will those on the left do? The Communists will do all they can to drag the other two into collaborating; but if they fail in this the Communists too will be shut out

---

Giuliano Vassalli. "Then there's a local Roman tripartite command and eight tripartite zone commands. There are also numerous militias, mainly out towards Tivoli and the Castelli."

and will be in serious trouble with Russia, which evidently expects them to be part of the government. If on the other hand they are able to drag the PdA and the PSI into a government, these three parties will split up, and the groups on the left will leave the fold and form a new left opposition party that will also include the dissident groups I will discuss shortly."

The text in fact then goes into a brief digression mostly about the three parties that don't participate in the Liberation Committee (CLN): "the dissident Communists, Social-Christians and Republicans." They "have formed their own 'Republican Federation' where they have 'no responsibility', and can therefore allow themselves the luxury of speaking frankly and conducting more straightforward and even-handed politics [. . .]. But some doubt remains whether this is not due to resentment at not being able to enter the Liberation Committee. Of course, this group is engaged in a bitter struggle against the CLN, and advocates its breakup.

"Certainly in the PdA and PSI," Eugenio continued, "there are also powerful groups that favor this breakup — but I can't say much about people in the PdA, because our friends there are very tight-lipped [. . .]. In the PSI there is a group of young people who hold all the strings of the organization. This group (mostly from the MUP and led by Ulpiano [Giuliano Vassalli]) contains some clever and interesting elements, although their formulations are still a little awkward. Their main concern is to attract to themselves all the elements of the left that are unhappy with PCI. So they are on excellent terms with the dissident groups of the Republican Federation [mentioned above], hoping to annex them one day in bulk; and they would favor the immediate break up of the CLN. I have been in full support of their position, but I do not feel I can fully support their mentality, which still seems mired in preconceptions. They are in any case one of the more interesting groups; they are open to new ideas, and will be the backbone of tomorrow's left. They are all definitely federalists."

23. These are notably revealing statements. In the form of a report (with an excursus), Eugenio intended to transmit to his distant federalist friends a set of important political assessments, culminat-

ing finally in a key judgment concerning this group of young Roman ex-MUP socialists among whom, in spite of some reservations, he had by then put down roots; and among whom (and beyond whom) he now intended to promote further developments, subjective and objective, in the actual situation — in a federalist vein.

Thus in the following section, *Federalist Movement*, after describing many of their activities,[113] Colorni wrote, "for around the last 10 days, and with the departure of our two comrades [Guglielmo Usellini and Cerilo Spinelli], the time has come to initiate some more specifically political action. With this in mind I have requested permission [from the party] to give only half days to working in the zone, and I will seek to join the editors of *Avanti!*. I think it's very important," he continued, "that a federalist newspaper should be released now. It shouldn't be so much a battle flag (like so many of the papers that come out now), but rather something contemplative,[114] looking at the big picture a bit more and studying Europe's general prospects rather than focusing attention on the Liberation Committee and whether or not it will come to power. The position it takes should in my view concern the following: Today's challenge is of course to work toward the expulsion of the Germans (and we are in fact committing everything to this), but this campaign is not an end in itself. Both the Communists and the PdA, precisely because they are linked in their ideas to two of the powers in conflict, forget that the point of the struggle is to be ready for the European revolution that will break out in a matter of months. The problem of power should not be posed as one of monarchy vs republic [. . .] but rather in terms of whether joining the government offers a way of leading the country with a firm hand in the European crisis accompanying the fall of Germany. This is the compass that we have to follow — not simply the institutional question."[115] Eugenio thus felt the need to

---

[113]Which we have already reported: cf. above, the conclusion of sec. 16.

[114]And thus quite different from what he had foreseen at the founding conference of the Federalist Movement — cf. above, sec. 14. Evidently the evolving situation had led Eugenio to change his mind.

[115]"In other words," the letter continues, "it is possible that even in a republic it might be advisable that the left not be in the government. Power under an English occupation would necessarily mean following an English policy line, and taking weak or strong positions in decisive moments exactly to the extent that this suited the English. Remember, the only card in

raise the level of the debate, proposing once again, in a federalist key, the notion of a European revolution. Evidently he would have liked to found a new newspaper, something he never managed to do.

On the other hand, even the underground Roman edition of *Avanti!* was in reality nothing other than a "battle flag," as shown by several brief editorial extracts from the end of 1943 that have been reproduced below.[116] We do not, unfortunately, have the elements necessary to trace Eugenio's hand in these different issues of the newspaper. We only know that beginning in November he actually took part in producing them, that he then became an editor and eventually chief editor.[117]

We do know, however, from a later letter-report — from 13 February 1944 — that at the same time, working with the young socialists of the "political committee," Eugenio started "a party school, which operated with great success. There were five courses: general principles of socialism, general theory of the state, political economy and Marxism, ideologies and political parties, and critical analysis of various revolutions. We will go on with this school as soon as the British arrive, preparing handouts for the courses, and I will be entrusted with organizing the popular university. None of the young people in our group are orthodox Marxists, and they are thus quite open to a revision of the principles of socialism in the direction that you propose. I have the impression, however, that the situation of the PSI outside Rome, and especially in Turin and Milan, is much worse than here, indeed all but a failure."

As far as we know, the didactic material Eugenio prepared for these young people is (unfortunately!) lost. If we could compare it with *The function of the teacher in Fascist schools*, a (truly remark-

---

a losing country's hand is the insurrection card, and we have to get ourselves ready to play it."
[116]It is clear that their embattled tone reflects a situation that hasn't yet been compromised and is developing in an atmosphere of national betrayal, the need for action and the expected arrival "of the British." It is also notable that only one article, from *Avanti!* n. 10, "Smuts' speech and European Federalism" [General Smuts, member of the British war cabinet], speaks of "we socialists and federalists."
[117]In fact, in a letter of 13 February 1944 to Altiero and Ernesto (through Guglielmo Usellini) — cf. below — Eugenio wrote: "I have been assigned an editorial post with *Avanti!*, and it is not unlikely that in the next reshuffle they'll put me on the executive board."

able) booklet adapted from articles in *Nuovo Avanti!* from 1937,[118] here again we would in all probability see notable differences — so different, obviously, were the young socialist learners of 1943–44 from the students at the Giosuè Carducci Institute in Trieste, and so different by now was their teacher, who had undoubtedly expanded his role as mentor and older brother. But I also think it would be possible to find a surprising thread of continuity, considering Eugenio's incisiveness and pedagogical edge — a distinction, a passion even, that he had not lost in the slightest. . .

The Hardest Months

24. As we know, at the beginning of 1944, Colorni took the initiative of publishing "a very elegant booklet"[119] — A. [ltiero] S.[pinelli], E.[rnesto] R.[ossi] *Problems of European Unity*. Accompanied by Eugenio's famous and captivating "Presentation," and undersigned by *The Italian Movement for a European Federation*, it includes "For a free and united Europe. A draft manifesto" — that is, "The Ventotene Manifesto," as well as "Marxist and federalist politics" and "The United States of Europe and current political trends."

Why, it might be asked, did Colorni decide just then to publish texts which a few months before, in his letter to Altiero of May 1943, he had considered partly outdated, when he now had at his disposal the finely tuned, very convincing, number two of *L'Unità Europea* which we have discussed above?

Presumably, it was for a number of reasons. Because at the time "The Ventotene Manifesto" had been printed in Milan[120] and was

---

[118]Now in Colorni 2019, chap. 3.

[119]"That will be out within three or four days," he added — that is, 16 or 17 February. The booklet was printed using an underground press Eugenio Colorni had improvised in the Montesacro area with the help of Leone Ginzburg.

[120]The successive issues of *Unità Europea* were also printed elsewhere. "The third was printed in Bergamo and the other five in Milan. Eight issues were printed in all. To these must be added the Swiss edition of number five" (Rognoni Vercelli 1991, p. 86). "The collection of federalist writings edited [in Rome] by Colorni," wrote Piero Graglia (in Spinelli 1993, p. 34, n. 20) "was one of the most 'successful' underground publications to come out in Italy. According to a letter/report Colorni wrote to Spinelli and Rossi dated 13 Feb 1944 (cf. below), publishing it cost him 27,000 lire (corresponding to around 10,000,000 1991 lire; the index of multiplication is 364,091 [around 6000 of today's euros]), putting 100 numbered copies in immediate circulation at 100 lire each [about 20 euros] (to support

unavailable in Rome, and because the "booklet" was a tool that was
useful for pursuing the federalist initiative as a movement, in several directions[121] and it did allow Eugenio to launch a subscription
for federalist activities. It is also likely that the difficulties he had
encountered at *Avanti!* led him to consider the publication of *Problems of European Unity* as a federalist counterweight. And furthermore, it gave him the opportunity to write with his own hand a new
"Presentation,"[122] pressing several sensitive points — almost asking
the reader to note them and take sides. It is undeniable, moreover,
that in spite of its limits "The Ventotene Manifesto" was by then a
document of historic significance for Italian federalism which, with
some minor editing,[123] Colorni considered important for the education of the new socialist generations to whom he was unsparingly
dedicating all his energy. And of course he held out the hope of
opening a breach in the socialist leadership (and that of the Action
Party, the Social-Christians, the Republicans, etc. . .)

On the other hand, these reasons, taken together, point us in
the direction of a new perspective on Eugenio's "Presentation" and
on the whole "booklet." The reading of the "Ventotene Manifesto"
that emerges is no longer the traditional focus on its 1941 genesis
on the island which then (sometimes) adds that Colorni later wrote
the "Presentation." And nor is it simply a discussion of Eugenio's
"Presentation" aimed as exploring its meaning as such.

It is actually be a new reading that takes previous ones into
account, but in a certain sense represents a change of direction. By

the federalist movement); after the liberation of Rome there was to be another 'regular'
distribution of 2,500 copies at 30 lire [about 6 euros]."

[121]"With Giunio's [Cerilo Spinelli] help, I hope that for a federalist action we can bring in
the federalists of the PdA, who are swamped with work for their party."

[122]Which he seems to be seeking to justify in the letter of 13 February1944 (as if to head
off the possible reaction of federalist friends in Switzerland): "I had to write the preface
myself," wrote Eugenio, "because we were unable to get a copy of the Manifesto you published in Milan" at the end of August 1943.

[123]"Colorni," wrote Paolini (1996, p. 219), "modified the original structure of the document, reducing it to only three chapters, putting the first part of chapter IV, 'The revolutionary situation — old and new trends,' into chapter II, 'Postwar Tasks — European Unity';
while the second part of chapter IV would be inserted at the end of chapter III 'Postwar
Tasks — The Reform of Society.' Along with improving its style, Colorni made some small
cuts, mainly in the sentences referring to Communist politics in Russia and the concordat
between Italy and the Holy See."

focusing on the historical moment (objective and subjective) when the "Presentation" was written and the "Ventotene Manifesto" was published in what would be considered its definitive version, it is possible to gradually "absorb" into the reasoning the new perspectives Colorni had attributed to the main issues of federalism as well as the contributions to the discussion of his Ventotene friends (Altiero above all) — both in putting together *L'Unità Europea* n. 2 and in the May-July correspondence.[124] It is this, in my opinion, that brings the actual meaning of the publication into focus.

The fact is, Eugenio was not interested in offering what by then was simply a historical reference to federalism, much less suggesting the substitution of one ideological choice for another. On the contrary, what he wanted was to use his point of view as educational material, intended for cultural dissemination — material which in the light of the current situation at the beginning of 1944, would help to fine tune, either orally or in writing, important additional arguments (inferred from the "booklet" — through comparison and/or contrast) about the actual state of things, and about future perspectives. Which is to say, *Problems of European Unity* represented a "context" (close up, but interesting) that permitted an advance beyond the simple worries of the day (military and institutional). It thus (reversing the reasoning) made it possible to put today's issues in perspective — the key requirement expressed in the "Letter to federalist friends in Switzerland." And it was also a way of making himself understood and letting industrious readers know what their work ought to consist of.[125]

---

[124]Obvious limitations of space counsel against my embarking on such an exercise. But to be convinced of it, industrious readers may wish to undertake it on their own based on the elements mentioned so far and the corresponding texts.

[125]Might this be the reason these texts have been re-published so many times over the years (from Spinelli and Rossi edited by Luciano Bolis of 1979, for example, to Spinelli edited by Mario Albertini of 1985)? I would say partly yes and partly no. Yes, because reprinting *The Ventotene Manifesto* (with accessories and appurtenances) has always been useful in "putting into perspective," so to speak, the present state of affairs. No, because in a certain sense, the result of isolating the "Manifesto" from the critical discussions that have followed it, such as those of the 1940s (and at the same time from the key contributions of Eugenio Colorni) has been to simplify and even trivialize the message of struggle and hope that the events of the time have brought down to us — a message which, as I have been trying to show, must be pursued to its conclusion if it is to be useful to us in our thought

It was, in fact, an important publication, critical of all ideological stasis, and standing firmly on the side of the daily process of questioning, reconsidering, discovering and relaunching that governed Colorni's intellectual processes and which he intended (first and foremost) to propose to his readers/interlocutors.

The *post factum* surprise, in fact, is precisely this stimulation of others that Eugenio achieved with his "Presentation" and with the simple publication of texts that several months earlier he had considered partly obsolete.

On one hand, what he had done fell perfectly within the scope of revitalizing Roman federalist activity in general, and on the other, it was what Colorni needed for his federalist-socialist initiative — it was an unprecedented point of equilibrium that he had reached by taking careful account, if I'm not mistaken, of the needs and difficulties mentioned above; it was in its way, an escape route — a typically "possibilist" way of thinking.

"The 'booklet,' Colorni later wrote in a letter to Spinelli and Rossi dated 10 May 1944, had gathered a 'remarkable consensus' above all in the PdA and among the Social-Christians 'in those committed to building a socialist ideology free from the myths of Marxism.' Among the socialist leaders, however, the text was received 'with suspicion, like an adversary's book, while the young people read it with interest.'"[126]

What is of course immediately noticeable comparing Colorni's "Presentation" with the editorial extracts from *Avanti!* from the first months of 1944 (cf. below), is that Eugenio had not been able to "unblock" the fundamental thinking of his party — to convince them to doubt their convictions (except the one about doubting,

___

and action. Indeed, I will not conceal that an intention of no little importance in these pages lies precisely in the hope of favoring the "resurrection" of the most lively and promising, but unfortunately forgotten side of the whole affair.

[126]Pasquinucci 2010, p. 279. A curious detail is that unlike the copies of the booklet in the archives of the EU in Florence or in the library of the Resistance, Pietro Nenni's personal copy, annotated in his own hand on the first few pages (and kept at the Nenni Foundation in Rome), is missing the initials of the two authors of *Problems* (and thus of the *Manifesto*) on the title page, a sign that Eugenio had the foresight to print some copies without such an indication, perhaps to avoid preliminary discussions of a personal nature with the socialist leadership.

in Albert Hirschman's pointed formulation).[127] Nevertheless, having authoritatively affirmed (both directly and indirectly) his own federalist position, this allowed him to resume his critical assault on the traditional thinking of the PSIUP (and the left) — with the added participation of some young socialist federalists.

25. The impression we get from all this is that the decision in favor of the underground publication of *Problems of European Unity* with an ad hoc "Presentation" came during a relatively positive period, at least in Eugenio's eyes, in which he had effectively managed to develop and consolidate his federalist revolutionary influence, chiefly among the young.[128]

In addition, the publication of the "booklet" took place shortly after 22 January, the date of the landing at Anzio of the American VI Corps — a moment, unfortunately illusory, when the prevailing idea among Roman anti-fascists was that hard times were about to come to an end.[129] This political climate was also reflected in the above mentioned letter of 13 February, which reads (in part), "Since the day of the [Allied] landings [at Anzio], the work of the teams has of course intensified. On the one hand we use assault teams, and on the other we're preparing a mass action for the first crucial days and for the interregnum period between the Germans

---

[127]It is a mindset opposed to the proud and intransigent attitude that so often prevails among intellectuals and politicians — a mentality open to forming its own independent convictions based on experience, observed facts, opinions received; a key ingredient for the proper functioning of the deliberative democratic process. Hirschman 1995, chap. 9, 4, 5, and 7.

[128]And managed also, it would seem, to reinforce the MFE. "We are now nearing completion of a facility," his letter of 13 Feb. states, "that will enable us to print our own and other newspapers. (The plant belongs exclusively to the European Federalist Movement)." Apparently Eugenio was still thinking about a new federalist newspaper: cf. above, sec. 23. "For our paper," Colorni added in the 13 February letter, "we have all the material ready, but I don't think it's too important that we bring it out now in this clandestine period teeming with pamphlets, since it would look like just one among many and we would have serious problems with distribution. Especially since your book will be much more effective propaganda. I think instead that we ought to get ready to bring something out every two weeks in the form of a Fascist Critique, as soon as the British get here." Leo Solari has also testified that there was "an underground press organized by Eugenio Colorni" and the young socialists that published numerous underground Roman anti-fascist texts.

[129]Is it simply a coincidence, I wonder, that Eugenio chose to sign his "Presentation" *The Italian Movement for a European Federation* with the date 22 January 1944?

and the English."[130]

Of course, the wait proved to be in vain for months on end. Indeed, once the German troops under Field Marshal Kesselring had
recovered from the surprise, they stood up to the Allies and actually counterattacked, inflicting huge losses (as anyone who visits the
American military cemetery at Nettuno can still be see in person).
At the same time, not least due to pressure from the Allies,[131] the
Roman underground partisan apparatus intensified its presence in
the city, and this was unfortunately followed by angry but judicious
Nazi-Fascist repression.

While an exhausting struggle for position was getting under
way on the Pontine front, the Nazi-Fascist police in Rome found a
way to dismantle, gradually and not without cost, part of the underground anti-Fascist apparatus — including that of the Socialist Party. However, the young socialists, having no fixed place in the party
hierarchy, were much less affected by the Nazi-Fascist raids than
those within the traditional structure — this was another source of
the decision to rebuild the Socialist Youth Federation (FGS).[132]

---

[130]I wonder if this double impression of relief and eager expectation related to the publication of the "booklet" has something to do with the subsequent reception it was given within
the MFE. Of course, the somewhat deceptive moment just mentioned may have been (para-
doxically) useful in producing the tone of Eugenio's "Presentation" and his editing, which
then favored the reception of both within the federalist movement for decades to come. But
it is also true that the successive painful reversal, which we will now address, perhaps led
to the development of a process of abstraction concerning that time, and also to a reading
of the "Presentation" "in and of itself" (to which I also contributed from Eugenio's side:
cf. Meldolesi 2015a and Meldolesi 2019, p. 34-44). If this makes sense, then it becomes
clear (especially to me) that, following the logic mentioned above at the end of n. 126, it is
essential to build a closer and more convincing connection with the time when *Problems
of European Unity* was published (alongside the well-known link between the early texts
of Altiero and Ernesto and the "atmosphere" of the confinement at Ventotene in which they
were conceived).

[131]Testimony of an anonymous Communist partisan. Fondo Solari, Envelope 1 (cf. above,
n. 88).

[132]The group was formed, Solari recalled (1964, p. 35, 36 and 33), with support from
young people "from various related political groups. In a flat at Corso Trieste 199 in Rome,
a constitutive meeting was held to define, inter alia, the new organization's plan of action.
In attendance were Sandro Pertini and Mario Zagari of the national PSIUP directorate, Eugenio Colorni (who for some time had been the political and moral guide for a good part of
the young people who later joined the FGS) Matteo Matteotti, Leo Solari, Bruno Conforto
and Giorgio Luchard. On that occasion the national executive committee of the FGS was
established, consisting of Matteotti, Solari, and Conforto. Matteotti was appointed secre-

"During the underground period," Solari explained,[133] "the political characteristics of the FGS included four fundamental components. The first of these was internationalist and federalist, and more than the others reflected the influence of Eugenio Colorni [. . .]. A second and no less vital component [. . .] was expressed in criticizing the mythology of 'imported revolution' and consequently exalting autonomous action on the part of the working classes for the attainment of their own ideals. A third aspect was a more clear-cut oppositional stance when it came to solving the problem of the monarchy, and a consequent attitude of reserve towards the CLN [. . .]. Another basic characteristic stemmed from aversion to a formalistic idea of the split between fascism and anti-fascism [. . .] and the resulting effort of the FGS to provoke an objective critical interpretation of the fascist phenomenon." Clearly, for these remaining points as well (especially the second and third), "the attitude of the FGS was closely linked to the thinking of Eugenio Colorni."

26. In this way Eugenio's influence grew. In the letter of 13 February to Altiero and Ernesto he had already written of his "very active" participation with Giunio and Giovanni[134] in the "political committee" of the young ex-MUP socialists, and that "within the group we advocate staying in the party for now, and not giving up on the work of the teams. [. . .] We have continued to argue that the

---

tary general, Solari was assigned the task of overseeing propaganda and partisan activity, and Conforto was responsible for political organization. Luchard was to collaborate with Solari in editing and publishing the official FGS newspaper and maintaining connections with other youth movements." "The rebirth of the Youth Federation," Solari added, "came at the worst possible moment during the Socialist Party's underground activity in the capital. That spring the Nazi-Fascist police had increasingly been tightening the straitjacket around the PSI's military wing, which in a matter of a few weeks had lost its best cadres. Arrests came one after another. The sensation that the police might have enough pieces of information to discover the organizational centers that still had not been hit was a cause for extreme prudence. The Youth Federation, having a structure separate from that of the party and therefore not subject to the consequences of the chains of arrests, thus constituted an important resource for the ongoing active participation of the socialist movement in the Resistance in the Rome area." "Recruiting, facilitated by the leaders' long experience in the party's underground activity, was rapid and relatively widespread. In a short time, the movement was able to count over three hundred elements in Rome."

[133]Ibid., p. 47–48 and n. 1.

[134]Giunio, as mentioned, was Cerilo Spinelli. Giovanni I have not been able to identify.

problem of the CLN. and the monarchy is nothing but a pretext, and that the real, deeper disagreement [with the PSIUP leadership] is over whether the party should take on the task of simply muddling along administering the country in the difficult years that follow the war, or whether it should instead move in a revolutionary direction [. . .]. Naturally the federalist issue has been constantly at the forefront of this debate."

Now, however, with the situation worsening, these arguments were printed (with better structure, and some formal caution) by *Avanti!* in the 15 March issue. "There are some," the article reads, "who believe that the essential purpose of the authorities is to muddle along and lead our country out of the tragic difficulties it was thrown into by the war Fascism wanted; to eliminate this failed inheritance in such a way that the people suffer as little as possible; to administer public affairs so as to guide them gradually to a settled state; to build merit in the eyes of the victorious powers. Meritorious tasks without doubt, from which no responsible party, least of all ours, would wish to shrink. But limiting our vision brings with it a series of perspectives on the future of Europe that we do not hesitate to call reactionary."

So the argument had become explicit. But in Eugenio's circle there was not even time to celebrate, because shortly thereafter the situation came to a head. Acting against the *modus operandi* followed up to that time,[135] and against the views of many Resistance groups and the Allies themselves, a Communist Patriotic Action Group consisting of seventeen people belonging to the Garibaldi Brigade who hoped to spark a popular uprising staged the famous 23 March attack in via Rasella on agents of the Wehrmacht. On the 24th the German command ordered and carried out the appalling Fosse Ardeatine massacre, touching off a wave of popular execration. At that same moment, on orders from Stalin, Togliatti had gone ahead with the so-called "Salerno turn," which resulted in a new government, known as Badoglio II (22 April), with the participation of six parties of the CLN.[136] Obviously, in rough weather

---

[135]Cf. above, n. 88.

[136]This was made possible, as we know, by the mediation of Enrico De Nicola (with the

like this, marked by severe shocks (on the left and right) that came, ultimately, from the Communist Party, it was not easy to "stay the course." Nevertheless it did not stop Eugenio from carrying out and planning new federalist initiatives (cf. below, the letter-report of 11 May), defending socialist autonomy, playing a part in founding the Matteotti Brigade,[137] inaugurating on 1 May *La Rivoluzione Socialista*, organ of the FGS, and finally, publishing a valuable article in *Avanti!*, to which we shall return.

Developments on the war front were slow and tormented. The intention of the Allies in landing at Anzio was to detach some of the German forces from the Cassino front and to occupy the Colli Albani, blocking the retreat of the German divisions, trap them in a violent pincer movement, and destroy them. As mentioned, the operation did not go well. Along the fortified Gustav line the Germans were able to resist the American Fifth Army, while the bridgehead established by the VI Corps in the Pontine littoral was stalled.

In this situation the action squad of the socialist railroad workers was given "the task of monitoring German railway traffic to and from Anzio and Cassino and sabotaging it wherever possible. The sabotage actions produced good results, to the extent that the German command was forced to employ several hundred technicians and soldiers at the Roman stations to guarantee security, not only outside the city but within Rome itself."[138] On the other hand, even the regime, in a classified report,[139] allowed that bombs, hunger and war had by now shaken Romans' "faith" in Fascist Italy. "The mood of the population in the capital continues to be one of depression, public opinion does not seem favorable toward our German allies

---

support of Count Sforza and Benedetto Croce), which provided that on the day the Allies entered Rome, while entitlement to the throne would be maintained by the king, all his functions would be transferred to his son as Lieutenant of the Realm. This was in the end followed by the Constituent Assembly and the institutional referendum.

[137]In fact "following a decision of Eugenio Colorni, Mario Zagari, Matteo Matteotti, and Leo Solari, the first Matteotti Brigade was formed and all the elements of the Youth Movement were transferred to this new unit. The forces of the FGS thus had an effective military framework, albeit only modestly endowed with weapons and ammunition" (Solari 194, p. 41–42).

[138]Tedesco 2014, p. 168.

[139]Roman Central State Archive: M.I. DGPS (RSI), 1944-45, envelope 7: cit in Ibid., p. 170.

and resurgent Fascism, while the subversive political parties agitate clandestinely." Finally, on 18 May, the Allied armies broke through, both at Cassino and Anzio. The Germans were forced to retreat gradually to the north, albeit with the bulk of their troops. After so much suffering the liberation of Rome was finally at hand. In anti-Fascist circles in Rome people began to breathe fresh air again. At the same time, unfortunately, the hour arrived for denunciation, revenge, and last reprisals — the hour, tragically, that killed Eugenio as well.[140]

* * *

The Construction of a Perspective

27. "From the papers of the regime," wrote Francesco Gui,[141] "Colorni's political and intellectual portrait emerges strengthened in its precocious, steadfast, balanced, original, as well as courageous and farsighted configuration [. . .]. Though convinced of the need for collaboration among all the forces opposed to the regime, and even while committed to militancy alongside the other components of the liberation struggle — the Communists first and foremost — the professor remained entirely alien to the logic of those who saw the USSR as the country leading the world revolution or leaned toward a bureaucratic-repressive conception of power. This did not lead him, however, to retreat into factionalism, but rather to champion the potential of socialist *leadership* on the condition that it should take the long view (the European federalist revolution) and of course have the ability to mobilize the masses. And that was not all, considering that Colorni did not hesitate to express his dissent, both rejecting Nenni's idea of a united front and undermining the basis of the communist 'myth' [. . .], not fearing that this would

---

[140]In all probability, the dynamic of this tragedy, which deprived Italy (and the world) of one of its best will never be fully clarified. The fact remains however, that in Pietro Nenni's notebook, in an opinion shared by the great majority of Roman partisans of all backgrounds, Nenni pointed the finger at an ex-Gap communist from the attack in via Rasella who had subsequently become an informer against the leaders of the Resistance.

[141]Gui 2010, p. 296: "Colorni 'elemento di contestazione e di cerniera' nei documenti degli Archivi centrali dello stato" [Colorni 'critic and linchpin' in the documents of the Central State Archive] — communication to the study conference of 29 May 2009: cf. below, n. 144.

weaken the struggle or that he would suffer the retaliation of his allied comrades."

In my opinion this is a balanced, eloquent, and useful assessment, but only a beginning with respect to my wish to do justice to the political Eugenio — leaving aside the harmful pigeon-holing tendency I have mentioned elsewhere,[142] which currently (and unreasonably) contrasts the philosopher Colorni with the politician Spinelli. Therefore, also just to complete this line of reasoning, it is highly useful to focus on the judgment of an exceptional witness — Giuliano Vassalli. Even in advance of the important conference in Rome on the life and work of Eugenio Colorni (on the occasion of the centenary of his birth, 29 May 2009)[143] Vassalli's viewpoint began to emerge systematically[144] on 18 May 2004 at a discussion on the subject "Eugenio Colorni 1944-2004. From the war to the European Constitution."[145]

As an introduction to this small conference, Leo Solari, brilliantly mastering memories, texts and feelings, outdid himself in outlining an attractive and evocative image of "Angelo." In fact, after several people had spoken, the then-President emeritus of the Constitutional Court, Giuliano Vassalli reacted, declaring, "I can

---

[142]Meldolesi 2020, p. 18. Cf also the beginning of this introduction.

[143]"Eugenio Colorni from anti-fascism to socialist and federalist Europeanism" sponsored at Palazzo San Macuto in Rome by the National Committee for the celebration of the birth of Eugenio Colorni under the high patronage of the President of the Republic, with the patronage of the ministry for Cultural Heritage and Activities, the Representation in Italy of the European Commission, and of the Municipality and the Province of Rome. Giuliano Vassalli's testimony — "Remembering Angelo (Eugenio Colorni and the Roman Resistance)" appropriately opens the collection of essays that emerged from the conference (Degl'Innocenti, ed., 2010a, p. 111–14) and was also taken up in the works of Daniele Pasquinucci and Francesco Gui (ibid., p. 275–303).

[144]Itself the endpoint of a line of reasoning that had long been "marinating" — as shown in Giuliano Vassalli's remarks at the "Presentation" of the 1980 Viareggio Presidente Award (cf. above, n. 8), in which, among other things, he said, "there was truly in him [Eugenio Colorni] an innovative impulse, even within the flow of the great socialist tradition — there was an authentically revolutionary impulse that also arose from what we could call his heartfelt anti-dogmatic and anti-traditionalist position."

[145]This was a study day (sponsored by the Municipality of Rome III, the EuroSapienza Interdepartmental Center, the Italian Center for European Education and the Rome Section of the European Federalist Movement) that took place at the Department of Economics, via del Castro Laurenziano on the occasion of the sixtieth anniversary of the death of Eugenio Colorni at which I was present and the acts of which are edited by Maria Pia Bumbaca (Rome, Municipality of Rome 2004).

only be grateful to have been a listener here, [. . .] especially for the
extraordinary and moving reconstruction by my friend Leo Solari.
As mentioned, he is the author of a beautiful book on Eugenio Colorni; and here he has vividly recreated the vision expressed analytically in the book, arousing deep emotions in all of us."[146]

It was thus the "re-evocation" of Leo Solari that set the illustri-
ous socialist jurist's memory in motion.[147] "The memory I have of
Angelo," he continued, "is of a powerful fighter, a thinker, a man
who had contributed this fundamental commitment, and with it
his profound and analytic studies, his passion not only for mathe-
matics, physics and philosophy, but for the political ideas that were
fermented in the federalist movement at Ventotene and again in the
birth of the socialist resistance in Rome."

In spite of the "terrible memories" that, even at the conference,
continued to invade his recollections of the Liberation,[148] Vassalli
fleshed out in a few sentences the effective, spontaneous and convincing image of the final "political Colorni," which he then took up
again five years later at the conference of 29 May 2009.

We have two brief texts which I believe are worth looking at
side by side to illustrate what to me seems essential.

"In brief, fleeting encounters," Giuliano recalled,[149] "and in talks
that sometimes went deeper, you might say that I spent months with
Angelo, from the beginning of September to the day I was caught and
taken away to via Tasso, 3 April 1944. [. . .] I say September because

---

[146]Vassalli 2004, p. 39. The book Vassalli is referring to is of course Solari's *Eugenio Colorni. Ieri e sempre* 1980.

[147]"During the Roman Resistance (8 Sep 1943 – 4 June 1944)," Vassalli later stated (2010,
p. 111) "or rather during the first seven months of it (during the last two I was detained
[. . .]) I personally met Eugenio Colorni a number of times. He was a passionate scholar
of philosophy and other sciences, extraordinarily intelligent and pure of heart. Obviously
I had long been aware of his fame — linked to his underground activities during Fascism,
first with the Justice and Liberty movement and then with the Socialist Party and its affairs,
and finally with the European Federalist Movement, of which Colorni was the precursor,
protagonist, and promoter."

[148]On 4 June, the Liberation of Rome, Vassalli emerged from the notorious via Tasso.
"I can tell you," he added (2004, p. 40) "that the sense of freedom and the return to my
family" — he had a wife and children — "was almost overwhelmed in those days by what
I discovered" — the loss of his cousin, artillery captain Fabrizio Vassalli, shot; Eugenio
murdered; and the discovery of the fourteen martyrs of La Storta."

[149]Vassalli 2004, p. 39 and 40.

I seem to remember that in August he wasn't present at the Italian Socialist Party reconstruction[150] [. . .]. Colorni was for us a leader of the Resistance, a leader of the Resistance in the sense of a driving force. Colorni had a huge role in the formation of the Socialist Party in those months [of the Nazi occupation of Rome] — he was a sort of intermediary between Leo Solari's dissidents and the [young] socialist federation, and a part of the 'Initiative' group that I belonged to."

Eugenio's federalist orientation, as Vassalli had argued before, in 1980,[151] "undoubtedly sprang from a vision of future European and world problems that went well beyond arguments, bitter and important as they were, between fascism and anti-fascism, a view that saw behind fascist movements a constant and recurrent authoritarian danger wherever they came from, and saw the elements in anti-fascism that were seeking to grasp what was truly revolutionary. [. . .] His federalist idea itself," he pointed out, "came from an inspiration that was broader, you might say — an inspiration, a position in which Europe only represented the present moment, the immediate next step in a renewed vision of all international relations, a vision above all of a point that he never tired of emphasizing — the necessity of an alignment of a liberal and liberating position in foreign policy and international politics with a liberal, profoundly liberal position within countries and various legal systems. He denounced all state structures in their oppressive danger. There are liberal ideas that are absolutely fundamental in his socialist conception."

"Concerning socialism [. . .]," Giuliano later added,[152] "Colorni had a conception that was all his own, both revolutionary and full of innovative ambition. He was certainly neither communist nor communist-leaning, but he didn't rule out working with the party or its people — within certain limits. He saw in the masses a spontaneity akin to what he himself aspired to. He was inspired by youth movements and interests, whatever their origins, as long as they tended to converge on socialist positions. He was deeply

---

[150]In a certain sense — see above (sec. 13 and n. 64) — he was present behind the scenes.
[151]In the discussion at the "Presentation" of the Viareggio Presidente Award (cf. above, n. 8).
[152]Vassalli 2010, p. 113–14.

committed to democracy and held it indispensable in a just and civil society. [. . .] Undoubtedly his life during that last year, spent primarily in Rome [. . .] was extremely intense.

Thought and action were perfectly integrated. Colorni carried through with his thinking on the fate of Europe and the world and with his participation in Italian political disputes, and at the same time did publicity for the party and took part in partisan activities in the context of the then PSIUP, close to the Socialist Initiative and above all to the Socialist Youth Movement."

On the other hand, Vassalli recalled at the small 2004 conference, "I was not in agreement with them [the young socialists], as they know. I was more 'CLNistic' [closer to the National Liberation Committee], while they asserted their independence from the CLN and warned of its dangers — of a continuation of the past, a recovery that did not take account of all the innovation that would be necessary in Italy and Europe after the war, which was of course one of the reasons behind the *Ventotene Manifesto*. So Colorni acted as a channel, a go-between, even though he wasn't completely with them, just as he wasn't completely with us [. . .]. And he performed this task of connection, discussion, fine tuning of what was to have been the post-war socialist movement in a remarkable way, and he did it with contagious energy."[153]

"He went along with or at least defended," Giuliano later added,[154] "the dissenting arguments of most of the leaders of that tendency [the young socialists], who were not in favor of CLN policy, fearing a political failure and a return to the old mentality that would sink any truly revolutionary aspiration. He was *both a critic and a linchpin*."[155]

"I remember," he said in 2004,[156] "an almost furious scene be-

---

[153]Vassalli 2004, p. 40. In other words, Eugenio carried out his political affairs with the same mindset — that of the critic and the linchpin on both the federalist front (from the correspondence with Altiero to *L'Unità Europea* n. 2 to the letter to friends in Switzerland) and the socialist (from working with young people and taking a leadership role to his federalist and socialist theses). Similarly, he fought the intellectualist tendencies of the Action Party and the authoritarian tendencies of the Communist Party.

[154]Vassalli 2010, p. 114.

[155]Italics mine.

[156]Vassalli 2010, p. 40.

tween him [Colorni] and Pertini in Piazza Cola di Rienzo where they were arguing so loudly we were afraid they would attract the attention of some Fascist." "In my mind's eye," as he told it later,[157] "I often see the lively dispute he had on the street with [future President of the Republic Sandro] Pertini, in which he defended the so-called youths against the misgivings of the great socialist leader of the Resistance, who opposed the excessive independence of the group from the politics of the party and was afraid of a split. It was February or March 1944 and the dispute, even in the noise and traffic of Piazza Cola di Rienzo, risked attracting dangerous attention. They were the two contenders of the moment, men of great courage, both fugitives wanted by the authorities."

Conclusion: "I remember Angelo, this great scientist, this great scholar, this great freedom fighter also as a man who was exquisitely political, exceptionally able in political activity and propaganda and in the lessons he was able to teach us even though he was only slightly older than we were."

28. This is an important endpoint, and it leads me to pursue in the remainder of this section a better understanding of Eugenio's political trajectory, in the course of which he also managed to become "exquisitely political, exceptionally able in political activity."

First of all, it is not easy to fully understand Eugenio's teaching. And it is even more difficult to follow its theoretical-practical trail — assuming, of course, that this is what we want. It wasn't easy even for those closest to him, like his wife, Ursula Hirschmann who, after long and commendable efforts, ended up throwing in the towel; or like his close friends from Ventotene, Altiero Spinelli and Ernesto Rossi who certainly, for different reasons, did not fully understand him. Even his brother-in-law Albert Hirschman, to whom he was very close and who in my opinion was his only true intellectual heir, confessed to me once that only Eugenio knew how to "both say and do" — a unique admission (for a self-identified intellectual like Albert), which explicitly recognized Colorni's superiority in

---

[157]Vassalli 2010, p. 114.

this regard.[158]

I myself would never have started down this road; I wouldn't have tried to pursue "l'Eugenio" (as they say in Milan) with my ex-students and associates if I hadn't been "rerouted" ad hoc by Albert Hirschman himself (and unwittingly!). As for the young militants Colorni met during his Roman journey of 1943–44, they were undoubtedly attracted by his extraordinary personality, but they never managed to truly penetrate the theoretical and practical foundations.[159]

We thus find before us a character who is brilliant but not widely understood — a destiny that often strikes true innovators; and one who for this reason calls for additional investigation. Consequently, this book is first of all an act of "due diligence," as the jurists say, which follows (at least in part) a collective itinerary aimed in the end at identifying a perspective useful to "everyone." Moving beyond historical reconstruction, we must look for the theoretical and practical sense of such a trajectory for the era Colorni was operating in and perhaps for our own as well. This requires reflecting on some of Eugenio's key texts, uncovering the implicit pattern they underlie, and then trying to translate them for our own time.

First point. "An inquiring, restless, anti-conformist mind like Eugenio's," stated Leo Solari,[160] "could not [. . .] help but get down to basic questions in politics as in everything else. [. . .] The federalist conception, as expressed in the *Manifesto* and by Eugenio, came to represent an authentic revolution in political thinking. The extraordinary originality in it as compared with previous statements of federalist ideas lay in the conviction it was based on — that the unification of Europe should not be a complement to existing political views, but a rationale for the re-conceptualization, from a radically modified perspective, of all economic, social and political

---

[158]And of course it isn't easy for me either, if even after so much work I've now ventured into Eugenio's final year — and right after editing the first edition of his political writings (2019) with an introduction entitled "The Topical Politics of Eugenio Colorni" — a clear sign that the work must go on, we have to keep going, "tell all."

[159]In my mind, only Giuliano Vassalli — just mentioned — was able to grasp at a distance, albeit partially, the political greatness of this brilliant political philosopher, endowed with such truly unusual energy and drive.

[160]Solari 2004, p.20.

problems. This was especially true concerning the subversion that this idea brought with it of the entire set of political conceptions and claims of the movements on the left."

Essentially, at Ventotene Eugenio had found, "what he had also yearned for in his research in other fields — reasons for a general reversal of views in politics," and he wanted to put his general intuition to the practical test in an era when the World War contained in it the germ of a possible reversal of direction.[161] In fact, the revolt against the Nazi-Fascism and the nationalist and imperialist rivalries that had led to this enormous collective tragedy — and this was the political message of the Ventotene discussions and the famous *Manifesto* — had opened prospects of redemption and rebirth.

In other words, the political formulations developed at Ventotene and put into practice in the Resistance called for a great push for liberation among workers and intellectuals. This is what actually happened in the Four days of Naples. It is what was building in the Roman Resistance. It is what Eugenio, with his fighting spirit, was bravely injecting into the social fabric of the capital along with his young socialists. It is what would then spread like wildfire in the north-central part of the country and elsewhere. It was essentially a matter of intercepting an "immense collective wave that was slowly building"[162] and releasing the social energy being generated at the turning point of the war — from Nazi-Fascist repression to liberation. Albert Hirschman would take up the same theme in his concept of unbalanced growth, changing involvements and the creation and conservation of social energy.[163] Because in the last analysis it is true that great social movements release extraordinary energy; they permit us, as Albert once told me, to "recharge our batteries."

---

[161] As he had written to Ursula in a letter of 20 May 1939 (Colorni 2019, p. 65–66) Eugenio believed "and wholeheartedly, in 'discoveries'"; but he was perfectly aware that the definitive test of a specific discovery, like the European federalism of Ventotene, depended on its being put into practice.

[162] Spinelli and Rossi 1944; now in Spinelli, p. 23.

[163] Hirschman 1958, 1982, 1984, 1986.

29. *The second key idea* to keep in mind showed up in Eugenio's thinking, as we have seen above[164] in his letter to Altiero in May 1943, and stayed with him throughout the year that preceded his death. He made it clear that victory for the Allies and the Red Army would undoubtedly come, but that the politics the victors put into practice would also depend on the behavior of the populations of the defeated nations.

"In evaluating the function of mass movements and the free expression of the popular will in the present situation," Colorni wrote at the end of "Revolution from above?," his last article for the underground *Avanti!*,[165] "we must consider that the victorious powers themselves have made no decision whatever about what their political line will be concerning postwar problems. There is in fact no unity of opinion among them on this point, and even in their own minds they have conflicting tendencies. [. . .] It is into this still uncertain and fluctuating context, in the current delicate political moment, that mass actions must decisively move. Their purpose must be to influence public opinion, chanceries, military headquarters — to show what can be done and what cannot be done. A clear "no" from the people and from the parties that represent them can today be decisive in causing the re-evaluation of a situation and radical changes of attitude in the ruling circles of the countries that hold our destiny in their hands."

In effect, the point here is to *condition* the winning powers. In Colorni's theoretical and practical strategy, the federalist proposition (as an alternative to totalitarianism, nationalism, imperialism, war, etc.) leads in this way toward triggering social movements and conditioning the great powers. But if such a proposal is to be "brought into focus," in my view it needs clarification on three points.

In the first place, to assert that European (and prospective worldwide) federalization must *prevail* over other forms of political organization to the point of requiring, as Solari puts it, "the re-conception of every economic, social and political problem in a radically modified perspective," also means that even in the vast

---

[164]Cf. above, secs. 4–6.
[165]*Avanti!*, underground Roman edition, n. 18, 20 May 1944; now in Colorni 2017, p. 205-07.

variety of concrete situations, it is necessary to aim relatively *higher* than the level where the subject is presently operating (at a territorial and/or sectoral level). Because this creates openings (material and immaterial — in expectations, hopes, culture, reputation) and thus favors the release of energies (rather than vice versa).

On the other hand, all of these conditions — but certainly does not cancel — other instances of politics that, though redefined, will continue to occur. For example — as mentioned[166] — in the discussion before and during Milan conference of 27-28 August 1943 on a federalist movement or party, this point was clarified when it was argued that the federalists had to agree concerning the European (and worldwide) federal option even while pursuing different ideas (liberal, democratic, socialist, etc.) in *internal* politics. So does this mean — it might be asked — that this point of view does not concern itself with internal federalism, and has perhaps lost contact with the Cattaneo-Risorgimental matrix of the Italian federalist tradition? Not at all — is the answer, because the reference to the Risorgimento in federalist writings by (and about) Colorni is ubiquitous,[167] and because by maintaining a common moving reference point this conception allows for a plurality of pro-federalist party positions and sets these in healthy competition with each other. In the same way that during the Risorgimento the prospect of national federalism certainly would not have excluded federalist experiments within the different states forming the federation, also in Eugenio's time the goal of Europen unity could have favored (and in its turn been favored by) federalist developments within the different countries. In other words — and this is the second clarification — the precedence of the external situation over the *internal*

---

[166]Cf. above, sec. 15-16.

[167]Cf., for example, sec. 12 above. As for European federalism, at the large conference at the Eliseo theater in Rome on 27 October 1947 organized by Ernesto Rossi, Gaetano Salvemini recalled (inter alia) that Carlo Cattaneo, after the revolutions of 1848 had been put down, "noting that the Hungarians had wanted to be free, but at the same time wanted to dominate the Slavs and Romanians, and that the Viennese had wanted freedom, but also dominion over the Slavs, Hungarians and Italians, added: 'Only in the equality of fortune and in the necessities of war could those vain people understand that without brotherhood there is no freedom, that it is better to be free brothers than resentful servants.'" (Paolini 1996, p. 599).

presupposes the existence of *external-internal* relations.

Finally — the third point — these elucidations are useful in qualifying the two main ideas recalled above, and in bringing out the main thread in the wide-mesh fabric of Eugenio's thinking. But in addition, they also suggest its overall *interactive* nature as a way forward.

On the other hand, it is clear that in the plans of the Ventotene federalists, the prospect of European unity represented the first step in a worldwide transformation — from a nationalist-imperialist system to a federalist one.[168] Now, in spite of the changes (and progress) witnessed over the last eight decades, I think it is clear that even today this fundamental issue isn't even in sight. We are still in a system dominated by great rival powers which in the absence of any sort of popular liberating and conditioning initiative risks the constant revival and even aggravation of its bellicose instability. This suggests two necessities — keeping the federalist argument alive as a guiding light (on pain of leaving room for dangerous outbursts of sovereignty and imperialist rivalry), and little by little reintroducing Eugenio's problems, *mutatis mutandis,* emphasizing the five liberating elements just mentioned: reversal, conditioning, prevailing, external-internal, and interaction — at all levels of the institutional scale: global, continental, national, regional, municipal, area.

In other words, precisely because they represent a discovery and are valid for our era in general, these five elements, with the necessary precautions of course (so that we can reproduce the original emancipating intentions, but attribute to them today's characteristics), can take on a specific meaning, and therefore help us evaluate our own and others' relevant experiences along with the prospects that await us.

Down the generations these five points have stood as a joint frame of reference in which humanity, perhaps without even knowing it, has long been trying to find its way. And this search will have

---

[168]Indeed, to be more precise — according to the *Manifesto,* constructing an international state and achieving European unity are treated as synonymous: read it to believe it! Spinelli and Rossi 1944; now in Spinelli 1985, p. 30.

to continue until a mastery has gradually been achieved over the dominant nationalist-imperialist forces whose jealous rivalries and grand maneuvers continually put humanity's future (if not its very existence) at risk.

30. Just days after Eugenio's death the Allied troops entered Rome. As predicted, the German troops retreated across the city. Some attempted risings in working class neighborhoods were quickly contained. The old CLN politicians once again took the situation in hand. The federalist policy of popular armed struggle against Nazi-Fascism appeared to have had its day. But in fact this was not the case — what had happened was the prologue to what was to come. It was the heroic period that came to be known as the Resistance.

Moreover, traveling a tormented road, the theme of a united Europe was destined by degrees to take hold, even if only in part. And Eugenio's circle had a role in it: Leo Solari, leader of the young socialists of the time, and Luisa Villani, Colorni's partner, who kept him proudly in her memory, kept alive through the years a thread of continuity with the extraordinary events they had lived through. Albert Hirschman began his creative rediscovery, in economics and elsewhere, of Eugenio's lessons. As an official of the United States Federal Reserve under the Marshall Plan he fought alongside the pro-European group that reported to the State Department.[169] Altiero Spinelli and Ursula Hirschmann (accompanied early in the journey by Ernesto Rossi) favored a push from below by a "movement."[170] These were very different ideas without doubt, but all of them, directly or indirectly were part of the collective "atmosphere" that favored Europe's first architects (like Schumann, Adenauer, De Gasperi, Monnet) under the protective American wing. It was Eugenio's "possible conditioning" of 1943–44 that was beginning to take shape. . . .

To summarize, I find it useful to do a snapshot mental comparison between the final Eugenio and the early Albert. At that moment

---

[169]Cf. Hirschman 1998, Chap. 2. In this way, as mentioned — cf. above, sec. 3 — the insurrection from below fomented by Eugenio in his final year finds a surprising correspondence in the pro-European role, limited but important, of Albert Hirschman in the Marshall Plan.
[170]Only to convert in the early '60s, Albert told me, to possibilism from above.

neither of them had the slightest hesitation — they knew exactly
what they wanted to do against nationalism and against wars, and
they actually did it. "The hour of courage" that had moved Albert in
1940 to work with Varian Fry to save more than two thousand European artists and intellectuals surely came from the same place as
Eugenio's "courageous phase."[171] Eugenio and his federalist friends
offered the decisive step of a United Europe as the alternative to
worldwide nationalism, while in 1941–42, in Berkeley, California,
Albert was writing his first book, *National Power and the Structure
of Foreign Trade* which, as the title itself makes clear, aimed to put
the foreign trade of the great powers under supranational control.
"Why dominate?"[172] wondered the young Hirschman who had just
landed in the United States. "Why be dominated?" echoed Eugenio from the Mediterranean. We have to keep asking ourselves the
same thing. Indeed, we have to recognize that we haven't asked it
enough in past years. Because the present "denoument" of what was
(and is) smoldering in the ashes should prompt us to look critically
at what we have believed up to now.

Luca Meldolesi

One of the most important lessons of the analytical position that
guided Eugenio Colorni and Albert Hirschman lies in the possibility of the in-depth exploration of a subject as we go along,
by modifying the angle from which texts and events are being
observed. This is why, after the two books of *Excerpts from Political Writings and Correspondence* of Colorni's and the volume of
Dialogues between Colorni and Spinelli, I thought it was important to concentrate on Colorni's thought and action in *The Final
Year 1943–1944* (even though this requires the re-examination
of some of the texts that have already appeared in *The Discovery of the Possible*, Part III). Because it is precisely this incan-

---

[171]"One day [Colorni] said, 'In a man's life there are numerous phases: this is the courageous phase." Testimony of Mario Zagari (Solari Fund, Envelope 1, File 10). The corresponding chapter in Hirschman's biography is called "The Hour of Courage." I think it
likely that the two brothers-in-law spoke explicitly about this in Trieste in 1937–38 because
of the likelihood of a world war's breaking out in the immediate future.
[172]Cfr. Adelman, chap. 6.

descent period that witnesses the emergence of the *Genesis of a Perspective,* as the title itself announces, whose extraordinary prescience and validity remain with us today. And also because, re-examining the many theoretical and practical contributions Colorni made in that overheated political situation and documenting them with other federalist and socialist material that Eugenio knew (and sometimes fine-tuned), the last phase of his experience acquires an extraordinary degree of vigor, attraction and authenticity, and leaves us with a fascinating image of this scholar, champion and hero of the struggle for liberty.

— LM

For discussions and research assistance I would like to thank Eva Hirschmann, Mario Quaranta, Geri Cerchiai, Antonio Tedesco, the Pietro Nenni Foundation in Rome, and of course Nicoletta Stame.

Bibliography

AA.VV. (2004) *Eugenio Colorni 1944-2004. Dalla guerra alla Costituzione europea*. Ed. Maria Pia Bumbaca. Roma: Municipio III.

AA. VV. (2010) *Eugenio Colorni dall'antifascismo all'europeismo socialista e federalista*. Ed. Maurizio Degl'Innocenti. Manduria: Lacaita.

AA. VV. (2011) *Eugenio Colorni e la cultura italiana tra le due guerre*. Ed. Geri Cerchiai and Giovanni Rota. Manduria: Lacaita.

AA. VV. (2011a) *Eugenio Colorni federalista*. Ed. Fabio Zucca. Manduria: Lacaita.

Bumbaca, M.P. (2004) "Biografia di Eugenio Colorni. Fonti archivistiche e biografiche," in AA.VV. *Eugenio Colorni 1944-2004* cit.

Cerchiai, G. (2009) "Introduzione" and ed., Colorni, E. *La malattia* cit.

Colorni, E. (1944) "Prefazione" to Spinelli, A. and Rossi, E. *Problemi* cit.; now in Spinelli, A. *Il progetto* cit., 1998; and in Spinelli, A. and Rossi, E. *Il Manifesto,* cit. 1979.

____. (1975) *Scritti*. Ed. N. Bobbio. Firenze: La Nuova Italia.

____. (1980) "Pagine di Eugenio Colorni." Solari, L. *Eugenio Colorni*, cit.

____. (1998) *Il coraggio dell'innocenza*. Ed. L. Meldolesi. Napoli: La Città del Sole.

____. (2009) *La malattia della metafisica. Scritti filosofici e autobiografici*. Ed. G. Cerchiai. Torino: Einaudi.

____. (2016) *Microfondamenta*. Ed. Luca Meldolesi. Soveria Mannelli: Rubbettino.

____. (2017) *La scoperta del possibile. Scritti politici*. Ed. Luca Meldolesi. Soveria Mannelli: Rubbettino.

____. (2017a) *Critical Thinking in Action*. Ed. Luca Meldolesi and Nicoletta Stame. Soveria Mannelli: Rubbettino.

____. (2019) *Critical Thinking in Action. Excerpts from Political Writings and Correspondence*. Ed. Luca Meldolesi and Nicoletta Stame. New York: Bordighera.

____. (2019a) *The Discovery of the Possible. Excerpts from Political Writings and Correspondence II*. Ed. Luca Meldolesi and Nicoletta Stame. New York: Bordighera.

____, and Spinelli, A. (2020) *Dialogues*. New York: Bordighera.

Degl'Innocenti, M. (2010) "Introduzione a Eugenio Colorni." AA. VV. *Eugenio Colorni dall'antifascismo,* cit.

Graglia, P. S. (1993) "Introduzione" and ed., Spinelli, A., *Machiavelli*, cit.

Gui, F. (2010) "Colorni 'elemento di contestazione e di cerniera' nei documenti dell'Archivio centrale dello stato." AA. VV. *Eugenio Colorni dall'antifascismo,* cit.

Hirschman, A. O. (1945) *National Power and the Structure of Foreign Trade,* Berkeley: U of California P; 3rd ed., with a new intruduction, 1980.

____. (1958) *The Strategy of Economic Development*. New Haven, CT: Yale UP.

____. (1963) *Journeys toward Progress. Studies of Economic Policy-Making in Latin America*. New York: Twentieth Century Fund.

____. (1970) "A Search for Paradigms as a Hindrance to Understanding." *World Politics* 3; now in A. O. Hirschman, *A Bias for Hope* cit. 1971.

____. (1971) *A Bias for Hope. Essays on Development and Latin America*. New Haven, CT: Yale UP.

___. (1982) *Shifting Involvements. Private Interest and Public Action.* Princeton NJ: Princeton UP.

___. (1984) "A Dissenter's Confession: Revisiting The Strategy of Economic Development." *Pioneers.* Ed Meier, G. M. and Seers, D. cit.

___. (1984a) *Getting Ahead Collectively: Grassroots Experiences in Latin America,* New York: Pergamon.

___. (1986) *Rival Views of Market Societies and Other Recent Essays.* New York: Viking.

___. (1995) *A Propensity to Self-Subversion.* Cambridge, MA: Harvard UP.

___. (1998) *Crossing Boundaries. Selected Writings.* New York: Zone.

Hirschmann, U. (1974) *Rievocazione incompiuta,* mimeo.

___. (1993) *Noi senzapatria,* Bologna: Il Mulino.

Hobson, J. A. (1900) *The War in South Africa.* London: Nisbet.

___. (1901) *The Psychology of Jingoism* London: Nisbet.

___. (1902) *Imperialism.* London; Nisbet.

Lipgens, W. ed. (1985) *Documents on the History of European Integration.* Berlin: De Gruyter.

Meier, G. M. and Seers, D., eds. (1984) *Pioneers in Development.* Oxford: Oxford UP.

Meldolesi, L. (2015) "Eugenio the Innovator." Dossier n. 1, www.colornihirschman.org.

___. (2015a) "On Eugenio Colorni's 'Preface,'" Dossier n. 1, www.colornihirschman.org.

___. (2017) "Attualità politica di Eugenio Colorni. Introduzione." Colorni, E. *La scoperta* cit.

___. (2018) "Introduzione." Colorni, E. and Spinelli, A. *I dialoghi* cit.

___. (2019) "Introduction: The Topical Politics of Eugenio Colorni." Colorni, E. *The Discovery of the Possible,* cit.

___. (2020) "Introduction." Colorni, E. and A. Spinelli, *Dialogues,* cit.

Merli, S. ed. (1992) *L'avvenire dei Lavoratori,* Milan: Istituto Europeo Studi Sociali.

Monelli, P. (1945) *Roma 1943.* Rome: Tipografie del Senato.

Paolini, E. (1996) *Altiero Spinelli. Dalla lotta antifascista alla battaglia per la Federazione europea. 1920-1948: documenti e testimonianze.* Bologna: Il Mulino.

Pasquinucci, D. (2010) "La Prefazione del Manifesto di Ventotene." AA.VV. *Eugenio Colorni dall'antifascismo all'europeismo* cit.

Pavone, C. (1991) *Una guerra civile. Saggio storico sulla moralità nella resistenza.* Torino: Bollati Boringhieri.

___. (2004) "Intervento." AA.VV. *Eugenio Colorni 1944-2004,* cit.

___. (2010) "L'incontro con Colorni." AA. VV. *Eugenio Colorni dall'antifascismo,* cit.

___. (2015) *La mia Resistenza. Memorie di una giovinezza,* Roma: Donzelli.

Quaranta, M. (2011) "La 'scoperta' di Eugenio Colorni nelle riviste del secondo dopoguerra. Gli scritti sulla relatività." AA.VV. *Eugenio Colorni e la cultura,* cit.

Rognoni Vercelli, C. (1991) *Mario Alberto Rollier un valdese federalista.* Milan: Jaca.

Rossi, E. (1944) "Eugenio Colorni. L'Avvenire dei lavoratori," 15 luglio; now in Ernesto Rossi, *Un democratico*, cit., 1975.

———. (1975) *Un democratico ribelle*. Ed. Giuseppe Armani. Parma: Guanda.

———, and Spinelli, A. (1944) *Problemi della Federazione europea*. Ed. Eugenio Colorni. Roma; now in Spinelli, A. *Il progetto*, cit., 1998; and in Spinelli, A. and Rossi, E. *Il Manifesto*, cit. 1979.

———. (1979) *Il Manifesto di Ventotene*. Ed. Luciano Bolis. Roma: Centro Italiano di Formazione Europea.

Solari, L. (1964) *I giovani di "Rivoluzione Socialista."* Rome: Iepi.

———. (1980) *Eugenio Colorni. Ieri e sempre*. Venezia: Marsilio.

———. (2004) "La lezione di Angelo." AA.VV., *Eugenio Colorni 1944–2004*, cit.

Spinelli, A. (1984) *Come ho tentato di diventare saggio. I. Io, Ulisse*. Bologna: Il Mulino.

———. (1985) *Il progetto europeo*. Ed. M. Albertini. Bologna: Il Mulino.

———. (1987) *Come ho cercato di diventare saggio. La goccia e la roccia*. Bologna: Il Mulino.

———. (1989) *Diario europeo 1948/1969*. Bologna: Il Mulino.

———. (1993) *Machiavelli nel secolo XX. Scritti del confino e della clandestinità*. Ed. Piero Graglia. Bologna: Il Mulino.

———, and Rossi, E. (1944) *Problemi della Federazione europea*. Ed. Eugenio Colorni.Rome; now in Spinelli, A. *Il progetto*, cit., 1998; and in Spinelli, A. and Rossi. E. *Il Manifesto*, cit. 1979.

———. (1979) *Il Manifesto di Ventotene*. Ed. Luciano Bolis. Rome: Centro Italiano di Formazione Europea.

Tedesco, A. (2014) *Il partigiano Colorni e il grande sogno europeo*. Rome: Editori Riuniti.

Vassalli, G. (2004) "Intervento." AA.VV. *Eugenio Colorni 1944–2004*, cit.

———. (2010) "Ricordo di Angelo (Eugenio Colorni e la Resistenza romana)." AA.VV. *Eugenio Colorni dall'antifascismo*, cit.

Voigt, K. (1985) "Ideas on the Italian Resistance and the Postwar Order in Europe." Ed. Lipgens, W. *Documents on the History* cit., vol. 1.

Womack, J. Jr. (1967) *Zapata and the Mexican Revolution*. New York: Knopf.

Zangrandi, R. (1963) *Il lungo viaggio attraverso il fascismo*. Milano: Feltrinelli.

Two Letters to Altiero Spinelli (May-July 1943)[1]

[May 1943][2]

I

{Dear Altiero,

You may not like the letter I am about to write; it is meant to be, if not an indictment, at least an attempt to clarify the reasons for the dissatisfaction aroused in many of us by your actions over the last two years. It is a dissatisfaction you feel yourself, if I do not misread your acts of impatience, intolerance, and irritation, which strike me as those of someone who feels in a vague way that he has not entirely got into gear. In my opinion, the reasons for this inadequacy lie in two psychological attitudes that I will try briefly to clarify before putting things in more purely political terms.

1) Your "Pantagruelian" attitude, which you defined in your "dialogue on detachment" and your "autobiography."[3] It's an attitude for which I have great admiration and sympathy (I expressed this, in fact, in a "dialogue on death," which I never sent you[4]). It is one of the most exalted and generous of human attitudes. It is not at all, however, the attitude of a modern politician, of someone, that is, who wants to achieve certain goals. It is the attitude of the entertainer, the teacher, the person who exudes warmth, who only needs to appear and people will follow him. Undoubtedly, some politicians

[1]Letter published in Spinelli, A., *Machiavelli nel secolo XX. Scritti del confino e della clandestinità,* edited by Piero Graglia (Bologna: Il Mulino, 1993) pp. 190–203.
[2]The letter exists in the Spinelli Fund in two typed drafts that differ from each other in some parts. The first, indicated here as "A," is longer than the second, indicated "B," since it contains an introduction that is not present in the second copy. Copy A has no indications, while B has a handwritten note at the top, "Ready for printing." The title of copy B is "The practical implementation of European unity. A discussion among federalists," successively crossed out and replaced with "What forces are operating today in the direction of European unity?" Included here are the complete text of copy "B" plus the additions taken from the copy "A" put between curly brackets { }. Only copy A is signed. [note by Piero Graglia]. In all likelihood, copy "B," along with Spinelli's answer and that of Colorni published below (Eugenio Colorni to Altiero Spinelli) were meant to compose a mimeographed booklet, which never appeared.
[3]Cf. *Eurostudium3w* (July-September 2007).
[4]Now in Colorni, E. and Spinelli, A. *Dialogues,* ed. Luca Meldolesi (New York: Bordighera).

have been of this type. But will tomorrow's political struggles really present themselves in these terms? Will the masses in search of direction really turn toward this kind of political attitude?

You accepted this as an unproven dogma, as an implicit premise. You started out assuming that at the end of the war the floodgates are suddenly going to open and the waters will rush down and submerge everything. And you assigned to yourself and whoever follows you the task of digging the great channel that will guide these waters and make them once again beneficial and fertile. In effect, this is what happened in many European countries in 1918. Will it happen again this time? It's a problem I will address on its own later. I don't believe the possibility has ever occurred to you that things might not go this way. Because of a certain mental inertia that always makes us picture things in a way that will favor the fulfillment of our own prospects, you keep imagining situations in which the unleashed and disoriented masses are looking for a guide, a beacon that will light their way. And you correctly propose that you will be such a guide for them — with greater intelligence and impartiality, with greater attention and attachment to the concrete situation and the needs of the moment than the traditional parties are capable of.

But what if things don't go this way? What if tomorrow's postwar period doesn't present this fluid and chaotic aspect, this new primordial state where victory is there to be seized by whoever has the most open mind and the stoutest heart?

It's a hypothesis you've never even considered, it seems so absurd. Or you've considered it only to discard it immediately, rejecting the idea that the old traditional parties have the strength to channel the floodwaters into their old and worn-out furrows. But have you ever wondered if there might not be new forces much more powerful than the old parties, which are already irretrievably directing the waters into channels that are indeed well-defined? We'll talk about this later. But it is precisely your inability (which is obvious to everyone) to face this possibility; it is precisely your horror at a situation that is not "Pantagruelian" — it is precisely this that sometimes makes your words sound empty and tired. You have planted yourself in the middle of the current, you've built your embankments, and now you're surprised that so little water is swirling between them. You get irritated, exasperated: 'Quit your fussing, roll up your sleeves and get to work.' But the fact is that there where you have planted yourself there is hardly any water. The waters are rapidly opening channels further down, along other banks that carry them more or less in the same direction as yours. But you don't notice. Those banks are not yours. They're made of a kind of cement that you don't trust. So you prefer not to consider them; not to see them.

I wouldn't want you to confuse these accusations of mine with the accusation, so often made against you, of having a "dictatorial spirit." It's not this that I'm criticizing you for. It is rather this "fever for action," which leads you to imagine that you are always in a central position, when in fact your position is peripheral. It's not that your 'Pantagruelian' way is disagreeable or unbearable, or that it offends my sense of freedom and independence. On the contrary, I like it very much and it doesn't offend me at all. But it makes you fall into errors of perspective and make blunders — that's all.

2) The second thing I want to reproach you for is not so much a personal defect as having let yourself be dragged, almost in spite of yourself, into a sin that is very common among those forced to practice politics in prison, confinement or exile. It is what I would call the sin of "ideology." I have recently had occasion to observe this first hand in people who had made politics the only reason for their existence. They had the same defects and shortcomings that we have so often criticized and laughed at in philosophers. They too built themselves beautiful palaces where they put everything they required, all their "needs," all their "ideals of civilization." For them too, the main worry was whether the palace would stand up in its logical coherence, in its "circularity." A political ideology and a philosophical system are in this sense like two peas in a pod. The aim in one case is to reconcile in dialectic harmony being and becoming, freedom and necessity, the finite and the infinite; and in the other freedom and authority, socialism and democracy, etc. You yourself have noted with a certain irony that for some time our politicians have been trying to find the right dosages of these things; but you too, perhaps drawn in by your arguments with them, have in the end not been doing anything different. You too are looking for the formula that will overcome Marxism. You too want to give the word socialism its most correct and modern

definition; you too are preparing your socialist sauce seasoned with liberalism to enter in the competition with the others. Not that these things aren't important, but right now they strike me as a bit abstract. And just as philosophy does not make progress by resolving eternal problems, but rather by rigorously meditating on particular facts, procedures and methods, and leaving the general systemic position in the background, deliberately inaccurate and only hinted at; so also politics, in my view, will not move forward by retouching its ideological structure, setting out the formulations and solutions for eternal problems; but by keeping its eye on developing events and trying to influence them using the most effective and unbiased methods; always, of course, in the light of some basic positions which it should be enough to have clear in one's heart and, I would say, in one's instincts, without needing to bend all your efforts toward giving them a clear and exact and logical formulation.

At this point I can hear you sigh with irritation at my eternal psychologizing, and appeal to me to talk about concrete problems and not states of mind. And that is exactly what I'm about to do. This preamble was not intended as anything more than the premise for a series of political observations}.

Dear Altiero, I would like to clarify some points of disagreement between us concerning the position to be adopted regarding the events that may occur in the near future. Many things have changed since our discussions of two years ago. I will enumerate for you some things that over the last two years I don't think you have given sufficient consideration to {you have noticed}.

{3) I said in part 1 that} The implicit premise of your whole political edifice is that at the end of this war the masses will run wild in movements that are violent and disorderly; and that the political victory will go to whoever can gain their favor and direct the force of these movements toward a clear and determined end. You stand out from the other parties in your desire to review and update the old ideologies and your lack of trust in old battle lines and slogans. But what you have in common with them is your method of fighting, which consists of going before the people, getting them to follow you, and throwing the weight of this approval into the political struggle. In this sense you maintain (always implicitly) that nothing has changed since 1918. You imagine that now, as then, the postwar period will be marked by enormous fluctuations in popular favor, following this or that man, this or that ideology.

Is it now paradoxical to think that this is not the way things will go? It is so only for those who want to see nothing more in the situation than their own desires and habitual ways of thinking.

The victorious nations of the last war tried to dominate the defeated states through territorial mutilation, military restrictions, economic and financial burdens. But they were not remotely concerned with influencing domestic politics. Germany, Austria, Turkey, Greece, and Italy were left in the grip of their own internal upheavals, "free," as it was put at the time, "to choose the regime they thought suitable."

The only attempt to intervene was in Russian politics, and this was utterly without success. The principle of "non intervention" was part of inter-war political morals, and it was the fascists first and then the communists who set it aside in the Spanish war.

Now I don't know how the winners will treat the losers at the end of this war. But one thing I do know for sure — this time they will not make the mistake of staying out of domestic politics. Intentions are very clear on this point; and not a day goes by when they are not reaffirmed by all parties involved. They want to destroy the fascist regimes once and for all, and no resurgence of nationalisms, chauvinisms, etc. will be countenanced. The distinctively ideological character of this war is what guarantees that the victorious states will not leave the losers to their own devices. And this will also be the weapon they use to fight against each other, each trying to gain influence over the other and cement its own predominance in Europe. Each of the two winners has a special apparatus for this purpose, and to achieve their aims they are ready to implement the powerful tools of propaganda, police, and espionage, along with economic and military intimidation.

As a result, the political life of all the peoples of Europe will be dominated by this factor, which will decisively influence mass movements and give them a very special character that they did not have at the end of the other war. This time we are in the presence of two very powerful state organizations that present themselves as paladins of the two basic ideologies contending for the European field.

Fighting for one of these ideologies will mean, not only implicitly but in the general consciousness of the people, fighting in favour of the corresponding power. The communism-democracy antithesis has gradually transformed itself into a Russia-England antithesis.

Is this good or bad? We will find out later. But it is a fact that would be foolish to ignore, and it will establish the ironclad initial conditions for the fluid and chaotic state which, as I have said, our mental inertia tends to represent to us as the immediate postwar situation. Once the great dikes have burst, the surging waters will not be free to flow in just any direction; they will be irresistibly drawn into the two huge conduits that are being readied to receive them. It will be in our power to help deviate them from one to the other. But wanting to oppose this, or to act as if it didn't exist, wanting to persist in presenting yourself to the people in the old way in hopes of rousing them through the clarity and honesty of your vision and the courage and resolution of your actions — this may be desirable and agreeable; but it's as if you were fighting alongside Garibaldi, rushing headlong and bare-chested at the enemy in an age of machine guns and tanks.

It is a historical phenomenon of tremendous import, representing perhaps the most essential difference between the 1918 situation and that of today. At that time the different ideologies, the different ways humanity wanted to configure its own existence, found their natural expression in political parties. Today they look to something stronger for support — the immense military, economic, political and organizational power of nations. Today there are three states (Russia, Germany, England) that represent in a nutshell the three basic types of political life known to our civilization. All three claim the right to organize Europe as they see fit. This war will eliminate one of them from the contest. The other two remain — and it is very likely that the struggle between them will not be fought — at least at first — with weapons, but rather with foreign policy, and even more at the level of domestic politics — each trying to attract to itself the various countries of Europe, maneuvering and influencing the various political currents in them, creating blocs and counter-blocs. And the various political parties will be nothing more than pawns in this immense game. Like it or not, it is in this sort of situation that we will find we have to operate.

2) {4} — Like it or not. The first reaction of people who think of a return to the situation of 1918 is not to like it. So they try involuntarily not to notice it. And if they do take account of it, they disapprove; they oppose it with all their might. "We want to be masters of our own destiny," they say. "We don't want to be anyone's protégés; we don't want to go along; we don't want to be the Quislings in this situation. If Europe is to be created, it will be by the will of Europeans, not by the ambition of this or that victorious nation."

Let us look at how things actually are. One of the most serious difficulties that arose when we began to conceive of European unity as the central postwar problem was to educate the masses and political parties to think and operate in international terms, rather than within the narrow limits of local and national problems. A European rallying cry — it was said — could have little grip on public consciousness, except during the very brief period of demobilization. As soon as political life returns more or less to normal, the masses will turn to the problems closest to their immediate interests; a prolonged education will be needed to accustom them to a broader and more comprehensive view of things. It was precisely this contrast between the urgency of the European problem and the public's unpreparedness to solve it that was the main problem for our program and the reason it was accused by others of being utopian. It seemed that a rallying cry that was international would necessarily fall on deaf ears with the public.

And now we are actually in the presence of an international rallying cry, imposed by virtue of its own strength, which presents itself to the masses as the only solution that is concrete and real and responds to the actual situation. We see it before us and we don't recognize it for what it is — are we going to reject it then because it is damaging to our autonomy and our freedom of action? We see that events themselves are taking shape more or less as we would have wished — do we nevertheless refuse to recognize this, only because it isn't happening in the form and style that we had initially hoped for? Only because things have worked out so that the forces we were counting on have so far had no role to play?

This rallying cry, whose power the masses today find irresistible — clearer, simpler, more elementary than any social or political ideology — is this: Russia or England. It is into these terms that the public translates, with confident instinct, every political speech they hear. I do not want to deny that this can arouse a certain melancholy. It betrays the widespread sense in the masses that the initiative has slipped out of their hands, that there are now more powerful forces deciding their destinies; it betrays their awareness that political ideologies have now become embodied in a well-defined state apparatus and have lost the liveliness and immediacy they once had. It expresses that sense of the passivity of the popular forces that has been so often evident during this war; that vague awareness of being tools in the hands of forces superior to them; only easy and thoughtless enthusiasm can lead one to imagine this disappearing at a stroke at the end of the war.

And yet, having said all this, the slogan is in fact typically "European." It is seen as common sense by all the peoples of Europe. It expresses an awareness that postwar problems will be solved at an international level; it identifies two powerful centers of unification for our continent. Trying to deny that the presence of this slogan in the conciousness of the masses represents a huge step forward on the road to European unity means not seeing beyond your own nose. This step forward happened in a very different way from what we had imagined. Our sort of upbringing and culture had no part in it. But if we have indeed decided, and not as a joke, to put the problem of European unity at the center of our efforts, we will have to acknowledge this reality as it exists, and base ourselves on it as a positive element pointing the way we have to march. Thinking in a European sense means first of all moving the center of one's vision.

Europe today is not an undifferentiated mass such that a unifying center could be indiscriminately created just anywhere. These centers exist in well-defined places, visible to all. We need their backing if we do not want to fall once again into nationalistic particularism or empty utopianism.

In the Europe of today, Italy has a strange, peripheral position, which can nevertheless be decisive for unification. Anyone who wants to take action in Italy must accept this position, and cannot behave as if we were at the center, the starting point of the movement, or as if the center could be anywhere. "But in that case," you say, "what should we do? Wait for others to take the initiative and then politely support it? Try to more or less subtly influence the ruling classes of the winning states, so that they happily accept their role as the initiators of a European unity that favors their interests?" I would now like to show you that this is not what we're talking about.

3) {5} — There is yet another thing I'm afraid you are not sufficiently aware of. Two years ago, when we were thinking about the unity of Europe, it presented itself as a goal to be reached in a single leap, in the period immediately after the cessation of hostilities. "It is essential," we said, "that we not wait for the hot lava to re-solidify in the old molds. We need to strike while the iron is hot, and see to it that when the victors sit down at the peace conference table to give Europe a new orientation, they find before them a Europe already launched on the road to unification by the revolutionary strength of its people. If we can't seize this chance at the opportune moment, we will have lost it forever; and the unification of Europe will have to be put off until the end of the Third World War."

This is more or less what we were thinking two years ago. Have the prospects changed in these two years? I would say they have. It's clear by now that at the end of this war Europe will find itself split into two areas of influence that are profoundly different in terms of political orientation as well as cultural and economic structure. What the line of demarcation will be, whether there will be buffer states between them, etc., we cannot at the moment foresee. Nor can we predict how the two winners will exert their influence on the states under their domination — whether by actual annexation (especially Russia) or by exercising political, economic and military control. In any case, it's clear by now that once the two areas of influence have been established, the whole postwar period will be dominated by an open or covert struggle between the victorious powers, by the attempted expansion of one at the expense of the other, and by their efforts to take control of key positions. The site of this struggle will be the continent of Europe, and clearly the people of Europe will not remain passive. On the contrary, the character of the contest will depend to a great extent on them — whether it will burn itself out in a simple imperialist clash between Russia and England, or whether it will be the starting point for the effective unification of the continent. One way or the other, what emerges from this perspective is that the struggle for European unity will no longer be limited to the narrow time frame between the end of hostilities and the conclusion of the peace, but will have at its disposal the broader postwar period. The last two years, I believe, have brought about this change in our prospects and made them vastly more concrete and feasible than they were before. Even here, events are moving the way we wanted, with or without us. It is a question of noticing this and taking it into account.

The two winning states, each the arbiter of a piece of our continent, have two paths open to them. One is a policy of housekeeping, of internal reconstruction, reinforcing the ruling class, repaying their own people for their sacrifices during the war by improving their economic conditions and promoting their psychological position as 'winners'; keeping the countries in their own sphere of influence in a state of economic and military semi-subjugation, covertly sabotaging any real revolutionary effort they might make, any attempt to clean house to make way for renewal. Or, there is the other path — joining with the vanquished, constituting with them a true and deeply-rooted unity; absorbing their lifeblood and civilizing forces; reconstructing together, sharing power with their ruling classes and letting them participate in leading the new unity being created; and facing the other half of Europe as a compact, aggressive bloc, endowed with an immensely strong power of popular attraction.

The two winners will oscillate continually between these two extremes. From a purely nationalistic point of view, the first option would represent a reinforcement of nationalist structures and would safeguard them against yesterday's enemies; but the second would allow very active and independent policy choices vis-a-vis the other winner, which would be prevented from extending its tentacles into the first winner's sphere of influence to try to break it up and win it over.

Even imperialist aims, broadly intended, might be advanced for either of the two victorious powers by a European policy. But certainly a decisive element in determining the choice is the concrete situation that is created in the countries within their spheres of influence. We can be sure, for example, that whatever desire for peace and domestic tranquility there may be in Russian leadership circles, they cannot remain disinterested if a widespread revolutionary movement should break out — as it quite likely will — in nearby

Germany. If the Germans are determined enough to take charge of their own destiny and impose on their own people this revolution they have long been ready for, the Russians will not be able to resist intervening and favoring unification. This will of course initially be under their direction, but it will soon give rise to a mixed class of leadership with a distinctly European character. In short, *it is in the power of the peoples of Europe to force the winning powers to come out of their nationalistic shell and to set in motion, even in spite of themselves, a policy of European unification.*

They will be able to create in Europe de facto states that the winners, in their own interests, cannot ignore. They can see to it that the situation breaks in one direction or the other. This is the high card in their hands. A card that will need to be played in actions involving the masses; not based on abstract federalist ideology, but rather stressing something people will be more than ready for — the fact that it is their attitude, every time, that can decide the outcome of a particular development in international politics, moving it in one direction or the other. Is this the action of a Quisling? In pushing them to act in our interests are we a fifth column in the winners' camp? I don't think so. It is more like the action of the men of the Risorgimento, who organized uprisings and movements all over the peninsula for the purpose of provoking intervention and making sure the international situation would come down on the side of Italian Unity.

4) {6°} — From what I've said, you can deduce what I think of the "European Federalist Movement." While participating wholeheartedly in the pursuit of its avowed purpose, I charge it with the defect of building the model of the perfect European federation too carefully, forgetting to observe the many outcomes of the drastic moves made by the countless forces on today's political chessboard — outcomes which, sometimes following unexpected paths that we could hardly have imagined, have served our own purposes. Only if we have the openness to recognize these formidable forces, and to embed our activity in their framework, only then will we get out of the field of noble ideology and into that of concrete action.

{Eugenio}

[July 1943]

II

Dear Altiero,[5]

Your letter has the virtue of clarifying the situation completely and leaves no room for misunderstanding. It is what I had tried to begin to do myself, and I'm glad you've continued it so honestly. Whatever conclusions we draw from our discussions, we will have reached them for good reasons and can be sure that we are not deceiving or deluding each other.

I am willing to accept almost all the observations you make in your analysis of the situation — I agree with you that "the revolution Germany has long been ready for" is nothing other than the communist revolution. I never meant to say otherwise. And your ongoing irony about the "inspired state of mind" of someone who sees this revolution as a "mystical event," etc. is lost on me, since I don't believe I have ever suffered from such a malady. I also accept what you say when you state that my judgment on the progressive or reactionary nature of Russia and England hinges on the support or hostility these countries offer the German revolution. It isn't sympathy or antipathy toward countries that motivates my judgment, but the ability I see in them to make up a bloc that might be the nucleus of a future united Europe.

I also agree with you that a communist revolution in Germany would strengthen "mass civilization" in that country at the expense of "individualist civilization"; and I have no illusions that "bringing about a collectivist transformation in Germany could completely change the German character."

And finally, I also agree that a Russo-German bloc set on the conquest of Europe would in all probability bring about a third world war (but, I hasten to add, it would truly be a definitive war for European unity, and not for European equilibrium like the two previous wars; it would be a war to achieve European unity now. In

---

[5] Letter of June-July 1943 published in Spinelli, A., *Machiavelli nel secolo XX. Scritti del confino e della clandestinità,* ed. Piero Graglia (Bologna: Il Mulino, 1993) pp. 213–18. This letter follows the answer of Altiero Spinelli of May 1943 (now in *ibidem,* pp. 203–12. For the date of this letter, cf. p. 173.

the Italian Risorgimento there were three wars. And I am not at all sure that to best implement and complete European unity a third war may not be necessary. Today the issue is to make sure that the present war constitutes a decisive step in that direction, and that we don't return to the status quo. That is, to make sure that any third war is not once again a war for European equilibrium).

As you see, our perspectives on the situation are more or less in agreement. It is concerning its solution that our viewpoints diverge. You insist on "individualist civilization"; I on European unity. You would reject a united Europe that was not based on "individualist civilization"; I would reject an individualist civilization that wasn't based on European unity. Just to avoid misunderstandings I will cite your words: "a Russo-German communist bloc would mean that the eastern border of Europe would return to roughly what was in Augustus's time. [. . .] Beyond the border collectivist and militaristic countries, bent on conquering continents, on this side countries that under Anglo-American guidance would convulsively try to save something of European civilization." Faced with the prospect of a Russian-German unification of Europe, your concern then would be to block it for the purpose of saving something of European civilization. Mine would be to facilitate it and hurry it along in every way.

As you can see, this isn't about political logic, or working out a line of reasoning down to the final consequences; it's rather that the situation, having become clear to a certain degree, imposes a choice that each of us must make according to our own leanings and sympathies, our own cultural and moral needs — a choice, therefore, that is very difficult to discuss with a cool head. What is clear up to now in our discussion is the possibility (if not probability) that we will one day find ourselves having to take a position regarding the prospect of a communist Russo-German initiative for European unification. I would go further — it is possible that the position of our country and the attitude of its people are exactly what might cause one side or the other to collapse — that is, either hastening a process of unification based on successive annexations or favoring a stiffening of western Europe for the purpose of saving "individualist civilization" and setting off the Third World War. We may find ourselves, one day not far off, facing this sobering responsibility. Are you really sure the decision you've made is already irrevocable?

It is somewhat painful, for reasons given above, to lay out for you the motives that prompt me to accept the prospect of a European union based on "mass civilization." I have done so on other occasions, in discussions that were not among our best. Nevertheless I will try to set down some points.

1st. In your essay "Marxist and federalist politics,"[6] you stated clearly that a collectivist economy is the only one adapted to a country at war, or in the grip of serious difficulties that threaten its very existence. And you also argued that a "market" economy contains within it no guarantee of its own stability, apart from assuring the development of certain social groups interested in maintaining it (I don't have the essay with me to offer a precise citation, but I don't think I've mistaken your meaning). Now I believe that a unified or unifying Europe will be obliged for a fairly long period to consider itself in a state of war, or at least a state of emergency. The make or break issue for this union will be the establishment of a collectivist regime. And if I'm not mistaken, your own argument with the liberals, and your clash with them, resulted from your assertion that the construction of Europe would require an initial period that was authoritarian, dictatorial, and collectivist.[7] The people capable of seriously and coherently launching such a regime are, by your own admission, the communists.

2nd. What makes you deprecate a communist solution, despite your approval of an initial dictatorship, is your position that for the communists, dictatorship and economic collectivism are ends in themselves; they are permanent methods of governance, not sim-

---

[6]Colorni refers to one of the federalist essays written on the island immediately after the *Manifesto*. His reference to "your essay" in the plural, which would seem to indicate the participation of Rossi in the drafting of "Marxist and federalist politics," simply indicates the extent to which the views of Spinelli and Rossi coincided in this period; things that the two of them wrote individually were often attributed to both. At the same time the distinction helps Colorni differentiate his own position from that of the two authors of the *Manifesto*. Cf. the text of the essay in question, written between 1942 and 1943, in A. Spinelli, *Il progetto europeo* (Bologna: Il Mulino, 1985) [note by Piero Graglia].

[7]Cf. Spinelli, A., *Machiavelli nel secolo XX* (Bologna: Il Mulino, 1993) pp. 115–23.

ply temporary expedients. Now I would argue that communism (especially a European variety) is much more capable of evolving than you think. I think it is unprejudiced in economic matters, and is thus far linked to a collectivist and autarchic economy in Russia only because of that country's frantic need to prepare for war. I think that even in the area of culture there would be a "Europa capta ferum victorem coepit,"[8] or at least that it would be our task — and a feasible one — to see that this happened. I am inclined to believe that the degree of "individualist civilization" in any regime does not depend so much on its institutional structure, its functionaries' goodwill or the ideologies that dominate it, as on the accumulation of difficulties and internal and external dangers that it finds it has to face. A regime in a state of war and in the grip of a serious economic crisis, or in a phase of unstable settlement can afford very little "individualism"; on the other hand "individualism" arises as a spontaneous bloom even in the most typically authoritarian and collectivist structures, once there is a relaxation of defensive tension and of the atmosphere of danger and struggle from which these structures arose. Look at Italy from 1930 to 1935. I think it would represent real conceptual and historical progress to get out of the habit of considering ideas such as "individualist or mass civilization" as categories to be used as evaluation criteria for an era or regime. This is a lesson I have taken from fascism which, now that it's about to fall, should not be thought of simply as a tumor that just needs to be cut out for things to go back to the way they were before. The criterion to be used today is "nationalist or cosmopolitan civilization"; and it is clear that even though both are totalitarian, the Europe of Hitler (with the caste division into Spartiates and Helots, as you so effectively characterize it) would be a nationalist civilization, while a communist Europe would represent a cosmopolitan civilization. Placing the problem of European unity at the center means having understood this shift in terminology. Placing "individualist civilization or mass civilization" at the center means remaining the prisoner of a pre-fascist mindset, and having practically given up on European unity.

---

[8]Europe, the captive, made her savage conqueror captive (Horace).

3rd. I have no confidence whatever in the "numerous and in-
fluential" men who "speak European" in England and America.
They will speak another language altogether as soon as they have
ceased to be part of the opposition. England and America entered
the war not to defend Europe, but to defend the European balance
of power. And there is only one thing that would bring them round
to an actual unification of their zone of influence — the danger of
a Russo-German unification. So I think your hope that "the war
will last long enough to shatter even further the internal resistance
that Russia might offer to a penetration of ideas and ways of life" is
a huge mistake. (Another mistake, incidentally, is that Russia has
been overwhelmed in the war only because it was attacked by Germany. Just think of the Russian-Yugoslavian pact in March). The
weakening of Russia would only encourage England and the United States in their reconstruction policy of creating "security zones"
against the danger of Russia and Germany, in fomenting enmity between them, etc. Betting on England alone as a determining factor
in European unity is letting yourself onto a slope that will lead you,
without your realizing it, into playing England's imperialist game.
Already, in your most recent writings, the problem of "individualist
civilization and mass civilization" has taken clear precedence over
the problem of European unity. And explicitly closing the door on
any Russo-German solution banishes the European federation into
the realm of beautiful utopias.[9]

---

[9]"I don't delude myself in the slightest that I have convinced you," Colorni continued
in a paragraph that he then deleted. "But if you will allow an old friend to make another
personal observation, I want to tell you that I don't like you at all in your new role as an
"individualist" and advocate of "western civilization." I liked you much better when you
confessed to an ill-concealed admiration for Hitler, when the reasons for your polemics
against the USSR were inefficiency, pusillanimity, and refusal to fight; when what dis-
turbed you in it was not the totalitarianism but their petty and mean politics. Now that these
accusations have largely fallen apart, you have retreated into the stronghold of 'individualist civilization.' It is an environment that seems to me not at all suited to your character. It
is an environment that is not very 'Pantagruelian.'"

EUGENIO COLORNI TO THE
VENTOTENE FEDERALISTS[1]

[July 1943]

Dear friends,

At the conclusion of a nearly plenary session it was decided that I should take over the direction of the movement. I hope to discharge my function to everyone's satisfaction. Our last discussions had caused me to fear that our shortcomings were too serious to allow us collaborate productively. But the articles you have sent, which I agree with almost completely (concerning the few points I have reservations about, all my friends here agree with me), clearly show that you also think the tone of the newspaper should be such that both our points of view are entitled to citizenship. This is the advantage of being a movement and not a political party. We can give the newspaper a generic character without going into the details of an issue. But for the main questions among ourselves we can produce mimeographed pamphlets — which I hope will be successful because they will showcase the vitality in our movement and the passion for ideas.

The leadership is constituted as follows.

Moreno[2] and Giunio[3] will work with me in the hands on editing of the newspaper. Moreno will also maintain relations with Milan, and will deal with people and parties and everything concerning the press. Giunio will be in charge of the distribution and dissemination of printed material. Turacciolino[4] will maintain contacts with you. Ostinato[5] will do the same work as Giunio. Pessimista[6] will be our representative in Milan. Minister without port-

---

[1]This letter was written two months after the Allies disembarked in Tunisia, and therefore before 25 July, from Rome, where Colorni had gone after escaping from confinement at Melfi. It was addressed especially to Altiero Spinelli, who was at Ventotene at the time [note by Leo Solari].

[2]*Moreno*: Guglielmo Usellini.

[3]*Giunio*: Cerilo Spinelli.

[4]*Turacciolino*: Fiorella Spinelli.

[5]*Ostinato*: not identified.

[6]*Pessimista* [Pessimist]: Mario Alberto Rollier.

folio, N. 2.[7] Ciccione Volante,[8] who from now on will be known as Eustacchio, will be the general secretary of the movement, working full-time. Naturally, these duties are flexible and can be shifted according to the occasion and need.

Political situation here: 1) I have recently had a long conversation with the main representative of the MUP [Proletarian Unity Movement], an old friend of mine from Milan. The MUP holds to the position of typical Marxist classist tradition. On the complete break between proletariat and bourgeoisie, absolute intransigence; they consider the PdA [Action Party] to be fascism in disguise, they reject any idea of a single front, and they would rather put up with fascism a little longer than collaborate with bourgeois parties. To my objection that on their own like this they will not bring fascism down, and if they get England to do it they preclude the possibility of having any weight in the future situation, he answers that England's plans will not be altered in the least by internal events in Italy; and in any case, he argues, England's influence on the destiny of the continent will be less than one might think. He agrees that Europe will be split into two great spheres of influence and that Italy will be in the English one. He predicts that Russia will have no interest in any sphere not its own, and will actually order communists to secretly boycott the revolution. The task of the Italian proletariat will thus be to make the revolution on its own. On the issue of European unity he says to think naturally, as he always has, since this goal has always figured in his program (that is, speaking plainly, he does not think about it at all). In general, he thinks there is nothing essentially new to discover — that the terms of the struggle are still the traditional ones.

My impression: It is a party that aims to exploit the PC's at least initially weak position in Italy, where they will be bound to accept English predominance and a democratic government. Thus the MUP will attract the discontented proletarian masses to itself. It may even succeed, if the communists are not more skillful than it

---

[7]*N. 2*: Ursula Hirschmann.
[8]*Ciccione Volante* [Flying Fat Woman]: Gigliola Spinelli.

is — but I think they will be more skillful, and that its will never be more than one of the eternal little groups of discontented socialists. Even now it's not the only one, and these groups will never get together for reasons of personal ambition (he says so himself). They hate the bulk of the socialist party, which they call the servant of the bourgeoisie. Having said all this, however, if England (as is possible and probable) follows a policy of reconstruction in Europe and Russia has no interest in the sphere of influence not its own, a party like this, if it can wean the masses from the narcotics fed them by the communists, may serve a notable function in its explicit refusal to accept a static situation, acting as an agitator in a state of affairs that threatens to congeal into "there is nothing to be done." But certainly today, with its ostentatious leftism and blind intransigence, amounting to what might almost be called electioneering, it brings to mind the pre-1933 German communists. With us, however, they would like to collaborate; indeed we have set up negotiations which, if they go well, may offer us an easy way to print our material. The basic idea here is that we will collaborate with anybody if there is mutual benefit favoring the underground work. This is essential if we want to accomplish anything; and we would ask that you do the same, eliminating personal friction as much as possible. Therefore, in spite of your prohibition, we will send you their answer to their comrades there; indeed, we request that you announce to them the forthcoming arrival of this answer and that you put yourselves at their complete disposal concerning the contacts they may need. You absolutely must do this — they have done us so many favors up to now (for example, they have greatly facilitated my stay here) that it would be downright ugly to refuse them this small service.

2) P.C.: After the dissolution of the Communist International it essentially split into two groups: the 1st of these, which still takes orders from Moscow and is looking for the largest support base (the king, the pope, anyone really) seeks only the destruction of fascism, peace, and participation in the future government. This last point is an essential condition for its support. Negotiations are underway in Milan for a united front composed of: Reconstruction, PdA, Socialists, Social-Christians, and Communists. The MUP has refused

to participate. This group of official communists now also includes some very well educated young intellectuals, some of whom are of the first rank, who without any experience or political preparation entered the party out of activist enthusiasm, considering this the party where there is the most to do (work among the masses, strikes, etc.). For now they are enthusiastic and extremely disciplined, but they make no mystery of their theoretical reservations (one of them spoke freely to me of the future task of intellectuals to combat "ignorance of Marxism") and do not rule out leaving the party the day they are no longer satisfied with it. They seem to represent a rather new type of communist functionary. Who knows if they'll let the party "squeeze" them or if they'll break away from it, or if the party will let them go on as they are. The 2nd group is the group of old communists who, for one reason or another, have lost contact with the center in Moscow; still seeing themselves as the truest interpreters of the Communist International, they want class politics and lean toward collaborating with the MUP. If I'm not mistaken, their position would be something like the position of "Gatto and La Volpe"[9] there where you are. Overall, the first group seem more interesting to me. I will see if I can make contact with them.

3) *The PdA,* after the recent arrests, is in a period of chaos. But I'm afraid you are kidding yourselves about this party as such. We can work very successfully among its followers (and we do so fairly profitably). But its most responsible leaders (I talked a long time with one of them before his arrest) do not believe in European unity at all, nor that England can be an initiator of it. Indeed, they think the English capable of throwing the *PdA* itself overboard and casting their lot with the monarchy and the army (but see the latest news). It seems that the Anglo-Saxons do not have excessive confidence in the Italian exiles and do not treat them very well. They refuse (it would appear) to appoint a nominal government committee, even in view of the invasion. This is evidently for fear of a repeat of Giraud-De Gaulle-Darlan, and because they don't want to tie their hands concerning how they will organize Italy after the war. You will

---

[9]*Gatto*: Camilla Ravera. *La Volpe*: Umberto Terracini.

say that this news is slanted; I merely pass it to you as it was given to me. We have excellent relations with the Action Party, as indeed we do with all the parties (except with the official P.C., with whom we have no relations for now) and several of our members are members of the PdA. For their part, however, there is some suspicion of us and a certain fear that we are deliberately causing disruption in their ranks in order to take away members. Therefore the stipulation that we are "a movement and not a party" is as timely and necessary as ever. Next to the MUP there is also a UP, which has a similar program and with which we also have relations.

I have just now had an interview with an exponent from abroad (France) of the so-called "Action Committee," a single front, established in France since 1941, consisting of communists, Justice and Liberty, and socialists from the Nenni and Saragat group. This person is clearly close to the communists and has promised to put us in contact with the PC center in Milan (he is also my old friend). This action committee included, for JL, first Trentin, then Lussu, who is now in Europe, and apparently also Magrini [and] Cianca, who is presently in Algeria; it had notable resonance in France among the emigrant masses. In Italy it was not widely known. Here it has now been replaced by the united front whose formation I have already spoken to you about. We will certainly try and join this united front and participate in it. It is a united front for immediate action to bring down fascism before the end of the war. In it, the PdA complains about the communists, whose channels are too broad and who would form alliances with anybody. Obviously, the PdA is worried about protecting its image as a non right-wing party and about possibly compromising contacts. Likewise, the communists complain about the PdA, which is reluctant to take concrete action and wants to limit itself to a press campaign. The communists, on the other hand, would like to begin an action of the kind the De Gaullists carry out in France, initially against the Germans in Italy. I am also of the opinion that we are at the point where we need to start to act. Moreno, who is going to Milan soon, will make contact with this united front and try to join it officially.

About two months ago, at the time of the fall of Tunisia, the question of a coup d'état was current for some weeks. Senators and

generals went to the king. The king took refuge behind his constitutional position — that is, behind the vote supporting the government in the House and the Senate. (In fact, the argument is not valid, because the head of government is responsible today only to the
king). It seems, in fact, that the king is highly devoted to Mussolini
and decided not to let go of him. Various generals commanding
army units spoke with representatives of the underground parties.
They stated that they were ready to act if the masses took the initiative. The party representatives promised the support of the masses
once the generals moved. So each was waiting for the other and
everything stayed the way it was. Apparently ammunition is being
taken from army units inside the country to be given to the militia.
It seems that for now the movement has quieted down. The prin-
cess of Piedmont is hugely active in the anti-fascist group.

Very latest news: Since the landing. Radio London has announced the formation of a National Front, composed of Socialists,
Communists, PdA and Social-Christians, aimed at the formation of
a democratic republic. This means that negotiations with the king
failed once and for all before the landing. This will greatly increase
the activity of the PdA.

Our work here: The 2nd issue of the newspaper will be out
shortly, and will include an initial brief on the action, your article on
Churchill's speech, an article entitled "Movement or Party?", an article on the dissolution of the Communist International, your critique
of the PdA program.

Please send us more articles of the kind that you have already
sent. And Pantagruel,[10] you should also send me a new answer to my
first letter, which could be published in a mimeographed pamphlet.
We would like to publish the entire conversation. In this answer, you
could include the criticism of the myth of German revolution and
your observations on the links between totalitarianism and collectivism, but modify the tone and make it more presentable. I also
enclose my answer to this letter. I would like you to let some friends

---

[10]*Pantagruel*: Altiero Spinelli.

who are there read my first letter — namely, Gatto and La Volpe, Ondeggiante,[11] Metafisico,[12] the one who had you send the poster to MUP,[13] Romanziere,[14] Biondo Ossigenato[15] and Violinista[16] (La Volpe's roommate).

Please confirm the arrival of the box immediately.

Attachments: Letter to Pipeta's[17] friend, accompanied by N. 2 (Pipeta's letter hasn't arrived yet). Commodus's answer to Pantagruel.

Commodus (Aldo from now on)

---

[11]*Ondeggiante* [Wavy]: Francesco Fancello.
[12]*Metafisico* [Metaphysician]: Riccardo Bauer.
[13]Sandro Pertini.
[14]*Romanziere* [Novelist]: Alberto Jacometti.
[15]*Biondo Ossigenato* [Bleached Blond]: Giuseppe Paganelli.
[16]*Violinista* [Violinist]: Mauro Scoccimarro.
[17]*Pipeta*: Manlio Rossi Doria.

Two Federalist Leaflets

Italian Movement for a European Federation

ITALIANS,

We didn't want this war, and what has happened in the last few days shows it. The fall of Fascism is only the first step of a long journey we must take with unity of purpose if we want to achieve peace and cooperation with other peoples.

Along with Fascism, many things must fall in Italy and abroad for Europe to be truly free. We must remember that there will be no peace and freedom, there will be no stable and lasting social progress as long as Europe is subject to the present absurd division into national states.

The only way to exit once and for all from this war is for Italians to collaborate actively in the foundation of an organization for European unity.

This will be the most urgent problem of the coming post-war period.

In the present moment, delicate as it is, the bases for its realization can already be set out.

We ask the present government for:
- Freedom of the press and free association;
- Liberation of political detainees and internees;
- Abolition of the special tribunal and racial laws;
- Expulsion of the Germans from Italy;
- Referral to the courts of the main perpetrators.

If we want to save Italy we must include our country in an effective European collaboration.

Rome, 26 July 1943

THE EXECUTIVE COMMITTEE

Italian Movement for a European Federation

ITALIANS,

The government's call for order cannot absolve us from expressing our thoughts and anxiety about the future of Italy. The war goes on, but how? By what means? With what chance of success? At what price in destruction and death?

Fascist tyranny has opened to foreigners the gates of a defenseless and disorganized country. There is no time to be lost! Either the new government immediately begins negotiations with the Germans for the withdrawal of their troops — and with the Anglo-Americans for peace — or else Italy will pay the ultimate price for Mussolini's political folly and will become England and Germany's battlefield.

Must we put up with this atrocious fate? We have to stop it with all our strength. The road to peace, the road to European Unity is signposted:

NAZIS OUT!

Rome 28 July 1943

THE EXECUTIVE COMMITTEE

L'UNITÀ EUROPEA

Agosto 1943   VOCE DEL MOVIMENTO FEDERALISTA EUROPEO Numero 2

UNANIMITY

Today the Italian people begin once again to think. They begin thinking at the most difficult moment of their history, with powerful forces threatening them, and it seems as if their fate is being played out in a game they can't follow. They had to sink right to the bottom of the abyss before they could find the genuineness and self-confidence they had lost. But our purpose is not recrimination. The reckoning will come in its own time and place.

What we have seen in these last days has given us a lot to think about. We have joined in unforgettable explosions of joy and enthusiasm from a people almost astonished to find the strength and ability to express themselves. But we have also seen lost and uncertain masses, unaccustomed to freedom, wondering whom to obey.

From this moment on we want to be perfectly clear: what has happened does not mean simply that the Italian people have changed their government and that this exonerates them from the responsibilities hanging over them. Today we find ourselves faced with elementary and exceptional problems whose solutions cannot be dictated except by the immediate consciousness of the people, even a people just released from servitude. Peace or war? Germany or the United Nations? Fascism or liberty?

We find ourselves at this crossroads in spite of the fall of Mussolini, which has not yet led to the fall of fascism in Europe, or even, entirely, in Italy. We must move beyond this crossroads as soon as possible, and there is no appeal to the difficulty of the moment, to the delicacy of the situation, to the diplomatic complexity of the negotiations, that can exempt our leaders from feeling bound by the powerful voice that surges from the Italian people today, crying

Peace, out with the Nazis, liberty!

In twenty years of fascism and vaunted "unanimity," there was never any unanimity truer, deeper or more immediately felt than this. And it is a great venture for the Italian people, at the moment when they begin again to be masters of their own destiny, to find themselves united in these aspirations, so simple and yet so decisive for their entire future. Nothing today is more important than these three things; and anyone who thinks they can slow them down even for a single instant so as to preserve established positions or to avoid disorder, commits a true crime of treason against the homeland.

The road to be traveled is long. But along the way there are some obligatory steps, things that must be dealt with right away without a moment's hesitation. This is the task of the present military government. This alone is why it exists, and only if this task is carried out will it have done a great service to Italy and to tomorrow's Europe.

It is not difficult to listen to the voice of the people, which is of course the voice that dominates the con-

science of every single Italian. The sooner Italy emerges from the absurd and tragic situation fascism has dragged it into, and the sooner it is able once again to show its true face, the stronger its voice will be and the more encompassing its right to take part in the construction of a free and united Europe.

It is not just today that we say these things. Our movement, born under the most ferocious fascist oppression, knows the hard life of illegality and conspiracy. Its people have long been accustomed to prisons and islands of confinement. If today we ask for the right to come out into the light of day, it is because we know that we are carrying our people's most deeply felt message and signaling the goal that, on pain of death, must be achieved.

A Parallel

The 1919 Treaty of Versailles left a Europe composed of 35 sovereign states in place of the 25 that had existed at the outbreak of the war, and consequently with an additional 11,000 kilometers of additional customs barriers. This fact alone makes it clear that the new European structure could not have come out less unstable than the previous one. The restrictive economic measures adopted by each state toward each of the others were progressively tightened to the point that the different sovereign nations had become so many watertight compartments. This inflexibility led to the adoption of the most absurd restrictions — monetary, commercial, migratory and even concerning tourism. Divided in this way, weighed down by enormous military expenditures and enmeshed in a web of restrictions of every kind, Europe could never have reached a level of prosperity comparable to that of the United States of America. This parallel is extremely significant. The United States constitutes a political-economic region with a surface area greater than that of all the European countries combined, excluding Russia (7,839,000 vs 5,275,000 sq. kms.). The unified market, with a correspondingly more rational division of labor under different environmental conditions has made labor in the United States vastly more productive than in Europe, which explains the higher standard of living of Americans with respect to Europeans.

What would conditions be like for these same Americans, on the other hand, if each of today's federal states constituted a market in itself, one that tended toward autocracy in the interests of greater security and was forced as a result into heavy peacetime military spending and periodic bloody wars over supremacy or disputed borders or some other issue? The Federation of 48 American republics is the fundamental reason for the extraordinary well-being of the United States and its citizens.

Dangerous Discretion

Regarding the imminent release of political prisoners, there is talk, from an official source, of senseless discrimination between communists and non-communists, between convicts and internees.

This shabby and craven haggling puts everything up for consideration except the torture of men who, after years of imprisonment and confinement, see their now inevitable freedom postponed day after day on pointless pretexts.

Do they really want to force us to publish the names and addresses of the fascist thieves and murderers who still circulate unpunished in our streets?

At the moment of going to press the news has reached us of the liberation of ERNESTO ROSSI, RICCARDO BAUER and VINCENZO CALACE. While waiting for our other friends, we extend greetings and fraternal devotion to those who after decades of imprisonment and confinement return to lead us in the work of rebuilding a free Italy in European unity.

L'UNITÀ EUROPEA

Agosto 1943   VOCE DEL MOVIMENTO FEDERALISTA EUROPEO Numero 2

CHARACTER OF THE EUROPEAN FEDERATION

In his speech of 21 April 1943[1] Churchill spoke of the need to bring into being under a global institution a council of Europe and a council of Asia. Focusing mainly on the need to put Europe in healthy order, since here "*lie most of the causes which have led to these two world wars,*" Churchill declared that this first council, "*when created, must eventually embrace the whole of Europe,*" and that while it must "*take as its foundation the moving spirit of the League of Nations,*" it will have to constitute "*a really effective League, with all the strongest forces concerned woven into its texture, with a High Court to adjust disputes and with forces, armed forces, national or international or both, held ready to impose these decisions and prevent renewed aggression and the preparation of future wars.*" It will therefore be necessary to work out a plan such that "*side by side with the great powers there should be a number of groupings of states or confederations which would express themselves through their own chosen representatives, their ideas concerning the organization of the council.*"

This is perhaps the most important federalist declaration made by the man responsible for the government of one of the countries that tomorrow will be in a position to contribute most to European unification. With this speech Churchill aims to accommodate the insistent requests of those British people who are most aware of the aims of the war. We can only be glad that the British government is starting to take seriously its role as a promoter of European unity, but along with all English people with European sensibilities, we cannot yet say we are satisfied with this first outline he has given of what the new international order should be.

* * *

When we talk about European unity, we mean a great and complex movement of spiritual, political and economic forces whose task over the course of the next few decades will be to bring different peoples together in a common effort of civilization that will erase the nightmare of new wars on the continent. For this vision to be more than a vague ideal, however, it is essential that we be aware of the need for an adequate international structure — and for this, even if it is not at present possible to set out all the details, it is necessary to have its fundamental features clearly in mind, or else the goal will not be achieved.

---

[1]This speech was actually delivered on 21 March 1943.

The tasks of the federation must consist essentially of guaranteeing international peace, ensuring free political life to all countries, abolishing economic autarchies and preventing them from being re-established, determining a single international currency, and abolishing colonial empires — that is, the exclusive possession by some powers of territories rich in raw materials.

To properly carry out this task, a federation — that is, a political unit that allows free peoples to participate in community life and does not constitute the veiled or flagrant hegemony of one state over all the others — must be founded on one basic principle. The degree to which we are able to free ourselves from imperialist patterns and from the politics of the balance of power and instead approach the idea of free cooperation between civilized peoples will depend on the degree to which the federation succeeds in applying it. The basic principle is this: the federation cannot be a league among states. It has to be a *res publica,* a commonwealth of all Europeans, who must, through their direct representatives and not through state ministries, contribute to the determination of the federal will; they must make contributions directly, and not through their state treasuries, to cover federal expenses; they must be called upon directly, and not through their state armed forces, to form a militia for the maintenance of order in the federation; and finally, they must be responsible to federal powers for any infraction of

federal law. In short, what must be created is real European citizenship — that is, a direct link of rights and duties between the federation and its federated citizens. Just as today, in addition to being citizens of our towns we are citizens of the state — bound, that is, by a set of rights and duties with respect to the state in addition to those we have vis-a-vis our towns, tomorrow we will be actual citizens of the European federation. This is essential, because only by applying this principle will we be able to create an organism that will allow the formation of a widespread European consciousness. Today there is no such widespread consciousness, and a federation will only become viable if it is designed in a way that will favor the development of one. But to achieve this it is essential that within the sphere of federal functions, the wall of national states should be breached.

* * *

A federal political body consisting of an assembly of state delegates would only ensure that federal problems continued to be worked out and decided in the closed space of state ministries, within the purview of the overall interests of this or that state. Nationalist groups would thus face each other compact, jealous, and wary. The voices you would hear would still be those of Italy, Germany, and France, and never those of the European classes of Italians, Germans, and Frenchmen who on many occasions might find themselves in greater agreement with each other than with their respective countrymen on certain questions. State representation consolidates national narrow-mindedness, while direct representation helps create an international political life that is truly the people's and no longer a diplomatic game.

Similarly, the collection of the taxes necessary for performing federal public services should not take the form of lump payments by the states as such, because this would make the whole system extremely fragile. It is not difficult to pressure an individual in default; but forcing payment from a defaulting state would involve an actual military expedition. And by the same token, if forcing obedience from citizens who refused to submit to federal law required going through the state police, the hostile attitude of a state would suddenly paralyze federal action in the entire territory. Fundamentally important are the armed forces the federation must have at its disposal for maintaining order. We will not have achieved our purpose if we are unable to establish that the military is recruited and commanded by federal power. Na-

tional armies must disappear in the same way that municipal militias disappeared before them. If the federation had to count solely or even mainly on national troops from the federated states, we would have, in the guise of a federation, the covert hegemony of the country able to field the largest army, which would follow federal orders only as long as its government didn't countermand them. Nobody could mistake the pre-1864 German federation, in which order was maintained by Prussian and Austrian troops, for a federation of free peoples. And as everyone knows, it came to an end with the clash between Prussia and Austria and the formation of the Prussian military empire.

* * *

The idea that establishing a federation means creating federal citizenship must be the compass that in the future leads us to accept viable solutions, whatever name they go by, and to reject those that, while perhaps prestigious in appearance, would be absolutely unsuited to development in the direction we want.

L'UNITÀ EUROPEA

Agosto 1943   VOCE DEL MOVIMENTO FEDERALISTA EUROPEO Numero 2

MOVEMENT OR PARTY?

We have heard this question many times in different contexts, from people of every political tendency and stripe. We would like to give our answer here and clarify once and for all our position and our intentions along with our actions and the point of pursuing them in the current struggle for the formation of a new political consciousness capable of solving the problems that the future poses.

Federalism — and we refer to it here without any doctrinal commitment, since its fundamental problems have been offered for public discussion in comprehensive writings such as "Manifesto for a free and united Europe," "Marxist politics and federalist politics" and others whose titles we are compelled for contingent reasons to withhold — federalism, we were saying, is a conception of peoples' process of development, based on the assumption — now tragically borne out by facts — that the era of national states is over, so that today we cannot speak of the internal order of nations, of progress, of social conquests etc., except in the context of an international order without which people and their communities become an instrument of imperialism.

Federalism is therefore a need that can be felt, and is felt, by people of every party, class, nation, race or religion, and as such goes beyond the traditional vision of political parties proper. What suits it best in this, its sowing season, is to be called a political movement rather than a party, since the need thus falls to the parties themselves as a first and most urgent goal, and the members can in due course belong to any party as long as its aims do not conflict with federalism's fundamental purpose.*

But to avoid any misunderstanding, it ought to be specified that calling it a movement suits federalism not so much because it limits itself to the task of building an internationalist consciousness (which is also among its aims), but insofar as it allows its members a certain breadth and variety of views towards social ideologies and government programs.

A movement — not a party — because, given its revolutionary conception and its need to unify, it conducts its activities at a different level, not in opposition, but parallel to what the various parties do, traditionally and structurally, when they pursue their struggle on national soil. Therefore the discipline that federalism imposes on its adherents is no less a commitment than it would be if it came from an actual party. Its character is thus quintessentially political because with regard to its objective — also vast and complex — it aims to mobilize any and all forces capable of working in its behalf, wherever they are found and under whatever progressive banner they serve. It aims to create its own organization, intent on spreading the federalist idea and remaining resolutely revolutionary in today's underground political life. And to lose no opportunity, in the legal political environment to come, to operate at the same level as the political parties and cooperate with anyone who, having reflected on the crucial interdependence of cultures, economies and the very lives of the peoples of Europe, perceives that there can be no lasting and valid solution unless — first — an international political structure is built that demolishes the remaining obstacles, annihilates resistance, overcomes mistrust, guarantees its own stability, harmonizes everyone's needs, and defends the true and profound meaning of the injuries suffered today against the inevitable reaction.

Making Europe will thus be the only way to save Italy as well.

L'UNITÀ EUROPEA

Agosto 1943   VOCE DEL MOVIMENTO FEDERALISTA EUROPEO Numero 2

FEDERALIST TENDENCIES

Due to lack of space we will post-pone until the next issue the publi-cation of federalist statements sent to us by various Italian and foreign sources, among which is a particu-larly interesting and welcome letter from our dear friends from the So-cial Christian Movement. We in-clude below a note of clarification whose importance and urgency may be judged by the reader.

* * *

There are many who have an at-titude towards the question of Eu-ropean unity that is still confused or distrustful. They speak or write about it without giving due emphasis to its importance. For example: they do not say that the resolution of the problem in a federal direction con-stitutes the *sine qua non* for any fur-ther progress and for the salvation of Western civilization; they do not as-sert, as they should, that the best-de-signed economic and social consti-tutional reforms within the scope of single nation-states would be sand castles if the European states failed to come together in a solid federal pact. Yet these reforms are the thing that really seems to matter to them, and they present them as achievable and valid objectives whatever the international order in Europe may be. They add the goal of federalism

at the end, just to pay lip-service to a "noble ideal" not actually meant to be translated into reality, not at least in the interesting period of political action we are preparing for today; just so as not to overly upset the "generous souls" still naive enough to believe in such an ideal.

This being the case, it is easy to see why on this subject they fall back on careful, moderate, non-committal formulas that any-one could subscribe to; they speak more freely about the formation of a 'unitary European consciousness,' than about the formation of a real 'European federation.' Who, we ask, could possibly refuse a request to do everything possible to build this consciousness, compatible with the actual situation that arises at the end of the war? But they consider it to be a premise *indispensable* to the con-stitution of a European federation of democratic states. Nonetheless, immediately following, they rec-ognize the need for an overhaul of international relations and values — an overhaul that would strongly deny the principle of absolute state sovereignty and reject territorial is-sues; they recognize, in other words, the immediate need for a juridical community of states that establishes and implements a collective secu-rity regime with adequate organs and means, protects minorities, and applies the colonial mandate fairly and progressively. We ask — what could this overhaul possibly consist of; what could the constitution of "a juridical community of states" possibly consist of if not the creation of a true federal order?

Lastly, they propose this overhaul and constitution in order to allow and ensure a general economic reorganization according to the principles of division of labor, the free transfer of productive forces and goods, and free access to sources of raw materials. We ask again — is there any system other than a federal one that would allow and ensure this readjustment of economic life? Why not speak more clearly? If it is necessary to construct European federal unity right away, this means that the formation of a unitary European consciousness is not the indispensable premise for achieving such a unity, since no person with common sense can seriously think such a formation can be achieved in a short period of time.

Our ideas on this point need to be very precise. Either you argue that the United States of Europe must come into being 'spontaneously' through the free agreement of all the peoples of Europe — in which case you limit yourself to a long-term task of propaganda and education and defend the principle of "non-intervention," opposing the interference of foreign governments in the internal affairs of any country — or you maintain that the United States of Europe must rise

in the period immediately after the war, essentially a work of the victorious powers — and in this case we must rapidly turn the international situation in the direction we want, provoke interventions and support the ruling classes of whichever winning powers will give us the most trust, so that we can help them best achieve a federal program.

We favor the second of these positions rather than the first, which we believe will create dangerous illusions and new disasters.

Widespread unitary European consciousness does not yet exist on our continent just as a widespread Italian consciousness did not exist during the Risorgimento. It was only the arms of Piedmont, Garibaldi, and the French that were able to bring about the 'miracle' of Italian unification. Attempts by Cavour and his successors to stoke popular movements that would have given at least a semblance of justification to the Piedmontese intervention were in vain. The plebiscites in the various elections were even less serious than the elections under the Fascist regime. And civil insurrections in the south spanning several decades showed what the people's real feelings were. Even then, a widespread Italian consciousness was not the basis — it was the consequence of unity. But still, the experience Italy gradually gained allowed our political life to develop in an atmosphere of increasingly liberal and democratic institutions right up to the outbreak of the next war, when no one any longer thought of undoing it.

If a widespread European consciousness does not yet exist, what does exist in every country of the continent is Europeans, just as Italians existed during the Risorgimento in the different regions of the peninsula. And the task of these Europeans today is analogous to the task the Italians managed to carry out at the time. They must give total support to progressive forces in those countries able to take on the role of initiators of European federal unity — in opposition to internal reactionary forces that support narrow and exclusive patriotism. They must take care that unity does not become a cover for the hegemony of the winning countries; they must, through cooperation, institute a new order that truly ensures equal rights and development opportunities for all groups of people within the general frame of common interests.

* * *

At the end of this war the situation that presents itself will be favorable as never before to European federal unity. But this situation will not last long. If we cannot make the most of it, if we let it go by waiting for the formation in all the countries of the continent of a European consciousness strong enough to express itself in the will of the majority of the population, we will give the old groups of sovereign states time to re-consolidate, and what follows will be the inevitable process of arms races, self-governing autarchies, and the politics of prestige and power until a new war breaks out.

But wars are not exams that people can continually repeat until they reach the level of political education required to pass on to higher forms of organization. Another war would easily lead to European unification in the shape of imperialist domination by the country with the strongest military. And with that our civilization would be suffocated and without hope for an entire era.

Eugenio Colorni to Ernesto Rossi

5 August, evening [1943]

Dear Ernesto,

Thanks so much for your letter. Concerning the question of whether or not to join the various parties, the PdA in particular, my opinion is as follows.

1) From now on I don't think we should present ourselves just as a cultural movement aimed at spreading the federalist idea among its groups, but as a political organization offering well-defined ideas. The fall of Fascism marked the beginning of an era in which European unity is no longer a distant ideal, but is present as a feasible possibility — and for this reason we have to be part of concrete daily political life, showing people how the words from the European unity guidelines are the clearest, most vibrant, and most immediately felt as responsive to the situation. This does not mean that we have to be a party — we do not in fact need to burden ourselves with a demanding program of internal, social, etc. policies, and we can tolerate divergent viewpoints concerning these problems; and also because the task we are proposing is not necessarily to take power, but essentially to act in such a way as to favor or bring about situations of international politics that take us in the direction of European unity. By now, our task should no longer have to be so much one of persuasion, but rather of real political action, making use of all the political means available (promotion among the masses, action within the leadership of the parties, contacts with movements abroad, diplomacy, the use of "myths" and popular "magic words" etc).

2) Having said this, a crucial question presents itself. Should our actions be carried out within the various parties, or should we turn directly to the masses in our own name? It is a difficult problem to resolve in the present state of affairs. But to make things clearer, we have to keep in mind that of the presently existing parties, from the PdA to the Communists, none has yet made direct contact with the masses, who have been effectively de-politicized by Fascism. For now, all the parties have a clientele composed of old pre-Fascist politicians and

people who have been working underground. But the real masses, who for years and years have believed that democracy and socialism were tired relics of the past (the only conviction that Fascism was able to instill in everyone, even including the workers) — the real masses, how will they react to the actions of the various parties of today? Won't they be disheartened, even nauseated by the tired old phrases on offer? Won't they be much more ready to accept the word of European unity, as long as it is perceived concretely — that is, as addressing the present, urgent problem to be solved, without too many institutional and social trappings? I believe they will — and in the few experiences I've had up to now in 'virgin' environments I felt an immediate response to what we had to say, much more alive and supportive than in the 'crafty' realm of politics. If this impression of mine should prove correct, then we ought to put our case directly to the masses, not using the various existing parties as intermediaries.

On the other hand, if my impression proves wrong, then it would be better to act within the various parties — not so much by putting forward a federalist program as by pushing them a little at a time to take positions and direct their politics in a way that we think will serve the purposes of European unity. Therefore, we should move toward assuming leadership posts, and not only in the Action Party, but also — at least — in the Socialist Party, since with the Communist Party we have no chance.

3) I would like to warn you against any excessive illusions you may have about the consensus your ideas have earned among the friends you speak with. They are old friends who love you and who are reluctant to contradict you, especially meeting you after fourteen years of separation. But I have very little confidence that they will actually follow you — perhaps by now they are already too busy with their own respective movements and groups. A typical example is Torraca. Not only has he never called me, but he was evasive in my three subsequent calls, each time putting me off to the next day and the last time even to the following week, so that I still haven't been able to see him.

I want to fill you in a bit on the work going on here. We hope to get Guglielmo and Cerilo out soon, but we still don't know anything specific. I went and saw Romani about them and about Altiero, and

by now the thing is sponsored from many sides. We are still distributing newspapers, fairly slowly. I'm sending you a pack of them with
this letter, and I've sent another pack to Turin (send me an address
for the movement in Turin and Florence). As soon as this distribution is finished I'm going to prepare a third issue that will include:
a background article on the situation (probably backing the war
against the Germans); an extensive article showing that European
unity is an urgent and very topical problem, and not a simple cultural idea (I will follow up on some ideas from my letter to Altiero);
your article demonstrating how the economic disadvantages of the
EU would be like inventing shaving cream without the razor; the letter from the Social Christians; and various odds and ends. Everyone
liked the last number.

I often see Rocca, who has sincerely taken your advice on board
and is fighting like a tiger to stay. Since Buozzi has taken charge of
the Industry Confederation I think they will kick him out, but he
says he has another solution in mind that might be good.

I looked for Olivetti today, but I didn't even get to talk to his
secretary. Apparently he's in Ivrea.

The people from the Social Christian Party are very kind with
us — they offer to work with us in technical matters (press, etc.)
and to take action together to get into the national committee, and
to stick to all our proposals. I am also in close contact with Rossi
Doria and Venturi, who propose to carry through with an effort to
rejuvenate the PdA. At this moment they are fighting to bring the
PdA into line for the struggle against the Germans. I support them
completely and we plan to hold a meeting of active young people
(together with the Social Christians, some members of the Socialist
Party, etc.) to prepare concretely for this.

Tomorrow I have a meeting with the Communists, at their request.

What has stopped completely after our friends' arrest is the
propaganda work, fundraising, etc. It's too bad, because it had got-
ten off to a good start. But we can't be everywhere.

If you like, I could come and see you at Monte Oriolo for a
couple of days so we can talk more easily.

I have a card now so I can travel.

A big hug.
Yours

I think the person we need to bring into our movement is Morandi. I would be very glad to speak with him, and if he should come to Rome, tell him to be sure and come see me. I think he would be interested in the way I see European unity and I would very much like to talk with him about it. Do I need to travel to Milan for this? He is an excellent organizer and one of the ablest politicians I've ever met. We worked together for several years. Anyway, tell him I would really like to see him and to know how we can set it up. I also really liked your suggestion that we look around for a while before deciding anything.

For solid financing you should see Att. Majno, who is very rich and generous. Get Ursula to introduce you.

Eugenio Colorni: The Socialists and the European Federation[1]

[September – October 1943]

Italian socialists want the peace that follows this war to lay the foundations of a solid united organization established in a Federation of Free European States. This entails the rejection of any League of Nations project which leaves the economic, political and military structure of the various states intact and offers a mere super-state in which single countries are represented with their full sovereignty undiminished, and against whose decisions any state or group of states with sufficient strength can remain recalcitrant. The only premise that precludes the possibility that political, economic or social achievements can suddenly be overturned by another imperialist war is the formation of a single European Federation with representative institutions whose members the citizens elect directly and not through the various states — a Federation that will provide a single market through a rationalized economic organization of its own, leaving to the individual states only the maintenance of domestic order. Such a Federation, while safeguarding national cultural and linguistic autonomy, will provide for the deep and intimate contact between peoples that should give rise to a renewed European consciousness.

Italian socialists believe that this prospect, one that might still have seemed a distant ideal only a few years ago, will come very close to fulfillment in the period following the present war, and are furthermore convinced that such a goal is closely linked to the objectives they pursue as socialists, given that the formation of a unifying European Federation is an event of such revolutionary importance that it cannot happen without the active participation of the masses in a thorough and general social renewal of our continent. For Italy, as for all the populations who emerge as losers from this war, such a solution would also be the only way to avoid

---

[1]Concerning the problem of European unity, during the period of the Resistance, Eugenio Colorni drafted this statement of principles, which later became the political platform of the federalist-socialists [note by Leo Solari].

defeat, territorial mutilation and economic subjugation. The Italian Socialist Party believes that it is specifically the attitude of the masses that will make the crucial difference in this regard. It will create situations on the ground that the winners will be forced to take into account, prompting action and pushing the international situation in the direction of European Unity.

N. 7   5 Novembre 1943

Avanti!

GIORNALE DEL PARTITO SOCIALISTA ITALIANO DI UNITA' PROLETARIA

THE PEOPLE WILL DO IT THEMSELVES

The resolution of the National Liberation Committee on October 16 (which we published in our previous issue) is destined to have the most beneficial repercussions on the political life of the country.

It is first and foremost an act of honesty and political integrity. Any collaboration of the anti-fascist parties with the monarchy and its minister Badoglio, even more than a political blunder, would have been a moral disgrace.

The country is now demanding seriousness and honesty from the parties. After twenty-two years of carnivals and charades, reaction disguised as revolution, variety-show warriors, and thieves feigning moral rectitude, the country needs to be led back to a simple, honest, austere political life, in which everyone can say what they are and do what they say.

The anti-fascist parties, by answering "no" to the invitation to collaborate with the monarchy and with Badoglio, foiling the machinations of late-to-the-party anti-fascists who hoped to be able to wash their filthy linen in the pure waters of genuine anti-fascism, have suddenly reclaimed the political atmosphere of the country. Their decision comes from a refusal to put up with small-minded quibbling. It says what it means — that the people, betrayed by the whole of the old ruling class, betrayed by Mussolini and Fascism, betrayed by the monarchy and the military leaders, betrayed by the plutocracy of the fasces and the swastika, intend to do it themselves, *they will do it themselves.*

EUGENIO COLORNI TO FEDERALIST FRIENDS IN SWITZERLAND[1]

November 1943

Dear all,

We haven't heard anything more about you or what you are doing, except the news that you're in Switzerland. Moreno[2] got out some days ago; since he would have scant possibility for movement and action here, we decided together that he should come to you, bringing with him as much news as possible. We are hoping that Giunio[3] will also be able to get out within days, using the same method as Moreno. I will now try and explain to you as clearly as possible what things are like here in Rome. I say here in Rome, because contact with Northern Italy is scarce and sporadic; and in any case my impression is that the political configuration in Italy over the next months will be decided when the English get to Rome.

The political-military situation. There are not a great many Germans in Rome, and so far they haven't carried out excessive acts of terror, apart from the deportation of the Jews, which was truly brutal. Evidently they are afraid of the Vatican and the various foreign embassies. They constantly circulate the rumor that all healthy men will be picked up, urging them to come forward voluntarily, but hardly anyone does. The city is full of people who live in a state of illegality (officers who failed to report, wanted politicians, men who have escaped from work service, etc.), but they circulate undisturbed and are not stopped in the street. The police have come looking for people at their homes (Pantagruel[4] and Giunio, for example, three times), but almost reluctantly, without pressure or excessive searching. Telephones are not tapped, even though everybody says they are. The Ovra[5] is not operating. On the other hand, there are numerous fascist informers

---

[1]Letter published in Solari, L., *Eugenio Colorni. Ieri e sempre* (Venezia: Marsilio, 1980) pp. 149–56.
[2]Guglielmo Usellini.
[3]Cerilo Spinelli.
[4]Altiero Spinelli.
[5]Organization for Vigilance and Repression of Anti-Fascism.

and many Gestapo agents who are operating, but they carry out their searches in Badoglio's military circles rather than in ours. Nevertheless, many arrests have been made in our ranks as well (Petronio[6] and Sara,[7] for example, and several others with them, but no excessively serious charges were filed). The police, the PAI, the fascists and the Germans operate with a certain amount of independence from one another. Nevertheless, all the authorities are totally compliant with the Germans, who give them whatever they ask for; and there are truly scandalous cases of criminal cowardice. The fascists are utterly miserable. Most of them are school children 16-18 years old, and they lack the courage even to mount provocations. Even the Germans despise them. They had announced big demonstrations for October 28th, and our teams were all set to react. But at the last moment, by order of the Germans, they didn't show up, so throughout the day we didn't see a single fascist in the streets, nor a flag on the balconies. They say the fascist squads have been dissolved and Pollastrini has been arrested and removed. They also talk about a falling out between Pollastrini, head of the fascist squads, and Tamburini, the police chief, who refused to put up with the fascists replacing the police. The result of all this is that the political parties are able to act with a certain facility, in spite of the difficulties and dangers. There is in any case vastly more political life than there was under fascism, even very recently. And there is a combative atmosphere that leads people to confront the dangers with relative cheerfulness. The underground papers are buzzing, the streets are full of anti-German and anti-fascist graffiti that the police are unable to erase completely, and each of us has a constant sense of solidarity from the entire population.

Military action by the political parties. Throughout the Badoglio period the political parties were unable to get anything from the military. They therefore found themselves totally unarmed at the moment of the armistice and, still worse, without organized teams that would have allowed them to participate in the struggle. All the same, some things were done, albeit chaotically and with no luck. Amid the total

[6]Sandro Pertini.
[7]Giuseppe Saragat.

disintegration of the army there was a feeling that the message of the anti-fascist movements had a strong grip on the masses; and mainly we saw what should have been done but hadn't. From 8 September on, we began working feverishly to avoid ending up in the same state of impotence when the next clampdown came; the first thing was the organization of the teams. This task has occupied all the organizational activity of the three parties on the left (PdA, PSI, and PCI), who have joined together in a "leftist bloc" in the Liberation Committee. What the prospects might be of this effort succeeding, even I — though I'm in it up to my neck — can hardly say. Certainly there has been notable progress right from the start. Many teams have been put together, the tripartite commands (that is, of the parties together) work well both downtown and in the suburbs; we can mobilize the teams quite rapidly; some actions have already been executed. But the most serious obstacle, one the whole organization has to deal with, is the lack of weapons. I think the three parties will be able to gather perhaps about two thousand men in the teams; but less than half of these are armed, and badly. How are these teams used? For the time being, only actions against the fascists are advisable and only these are carried out (especially against fascist spies). Actions against the Germans are allowed only when they leave no trace, because otherwise there would be reprisals that were too serious. What we mainly aim for are acts of sabotage. Many of these are planned and prepared; several are carried out. In preparation for an eventual state of emergency the city has been divided into eight zones, and these into sectors. The operating unit is a nucleus composed of three teams of 5 men each. A team has to stay together or be able to assemble quickly during an emergency under the zone command, jointly held by three commanders from the three parties, who will live in the same house. The actions to be carried out will be responses to possible looting, assaults on arms stores or food stores, possible actions of harassment against the German rearguards (apart from retreating troops moving through the city), and above all, during the interval between the departure of the Germans and the arrival of the English, the occupation of strategic points and important buildings, and the maintenance of public order, so that when they arrive they will find the city in the hands of party forces. There is a tripartite center (composed of Metafisico[8] for the PdA, Giorgio[9] for the Cs, and for the Ss, Petronio, replaced since being arrested by the person we had gone to see that day at the Villa Borghese cafe when there were no seats, whom we'll call Ulpiano[10] from now on). Then there's a local Roman tripartite command and eight tripartite zone commands. There are also numerous militias, mainly out towards Tivoli and the Castelli.

Political positions of the various parties. The Liberation Committee is composed of 6 members: Liberals (represented by Casati), Labor Democrats (Bonomi and Ruini), Christian Democrats (De Gasperi), Action Party (Lama[11]), Socialist Party (Pietro[12]), and Communist Party (Annunciatore delle Castagne[13]). The last three of these are united in the "leftist bloc"; there is also a unity of action pact between the last two. Nevertheless, the activity of the Liberation Committee consists of nothing more than a continual tug of war between the three parties on the right and those on the left concerning anti-monarchic and republican prejudices. On 16 October a motion was finally passed that seemed to bind the rightists definitively to the anti-monarchist position, but a short time later they themselves interpreted the motion in a way that left all possibilities open. What weakens the left in this action is the attitude of the communists, who are extremely accommodating, and the other two parties' fear that they will be isolated in the Liberation Committee. Nobody has the courage to take responsibility for the break; so we move forward with this behind-the-scenes disagreement that will come to the fore the moment the English arrive. What will happen then? There are two scenarios.

1) The parties on the left will successfully present a situation in the city in which they are its arbiters, completely undermining the authority of Badoglio and the king in the eyes of the English so as to get them removed (I am told that Badoglio has had little success so far in

---

[8]Riccardo Bauer.
[9]Giorgio Amendola.
[10]Giuliano Vassalli.
[11]Ugo La Malfa.
[12]Pietro Nenni.
[13][Herald of the Chestnuts]: Scoccimarro.

attempting to put together an army); in which case all six parties will come to power in a sort of six-person "Public Safety Committee" that will assume the royal prerogatives.

2) Alternatively, the English will leave the power with the monarchy, probably with a regency, in which case the three parties on the right will surely come to power; and what will those on the left do? The communists will do all they can to drag the other two into collaborating; but if they fail in this the communists too will be shut out and will be in serious trouble with Russia, which evidently expects them to be part of the government. If on the other hand they are able to drag the PdA and the PSI into a government, these three parties will split up, and the groups on the left will leave the fold and form a new left opposition party that will also include the dissident groups I will discuss shortly. This will seriously embarrass the collaborationist parties, especially the communists; indeed they are already lashing out against this idea, accusing anyone who favors it of being an agent provocateur, a traitor, etc.

There are three parties that do not participate in the Liberation Committee: the dissident Communists, Social-Christians and Republicans. They all would have liked to be part of the Committee, but they ran up against the opposition of their corresponding parties within the committee (respectively, the Communists, Christian Democrats and Republicans [PdA]). Now they have formed their own "Republican Federation" where they have 'no responsibility', and can therefore allow themselves the luxury of speaking frankly and conducting more straightforward and even-handed politics (regarding the Moscow conference, for example). But some doubt remains whether this is not due to resentment at not being able to enter the Liberation Committee. Of course, this group is engaged in a bitter struggle against the CLN, and advocates its breakup. Certainly in the PdA and PSI there are also powerful groups that favor this breakup — but I can't say much about people in the PdA, because our friends there are very tight-lipped, presenting things as if the party were in complete agreement about the intransigence of the republicans. In the PSI there is a group of young people who hold all the strings of the organization. This group (mostly from the MUP and led by Ulpiano) contains some clever and interesting elements, although their formulations are still a little awkward.

Their main concern is to attract to themselves all the elements of the left that are unhappy with PCI. So they are on excellent terms with the dissident groups of the Republican Federation, hoping to annex them one day in bulk; and they would favor the immediate break up of the CLN. I have been fully supporting their position, but I do not feel I can fully support their mentality, which still seems mired in preconceptions. They are in any case one of the more interesting groups; they are open to new ideas, and will be the backbone of tomorrow's left. They are all definitely federalists.

Federalist movement. Let me say that Breitarme's[14] accusations are completely justified. On 9 September I found myself, with only Breitarme and Eustachio, having to mobilize our forces for action. I put together a small team composed of about twenty people (the young people from the meetings that you attended as well), which functioned fairly well over those two days, doing what little it was possible to do. This team was associated with the SP, which I had joined as soon as I came back from Milan. In the following weeks it was clear to everyone that the problem of the teams was the most urgent, with the prospect of the British arriving in only a few days, and since my team, composed largely of Jews, had in the meantime broken up, and also because work with the teams required a serious level of organization, I decided to spend my time working with the teams in the SP. I was assigned a zone, which I still have, and Eustachio and I applied ourselves to various relevant initiatives. I was so involved in this work that I had no opportunity to engage with politics. But *quod differtur non aufertur,*[15] and now, for around the last 10 days, and with the departure of our two comrades, the time has come to initiate some more specifically political action. With this in mind I have requested permission to give only half days to working in the zone, and I will seek to join the editors of *Avanti!*.

I think it's very important that a federalist newspaper should be released now. It shouldn't be so much a battle flag (like so many of the papers that come out now), but rather contemplative, looking at the

---

[14]Braccialarghe.
[15]What is postponed is not abandoned.

big picture a bit more and studying Europe's general prospects rather than focusing attention on the Liberation Committee and whether or not it will come to power. The position it takes should in my view concern the following: Today's challenge is of course to work toward the expulsion of the Germans (and we are in fact committing everything to this), but this campaign is not an end in itself. Both the communists and the AP, precisely because they are linked in their ideas to two of the powers in conflict, forget that the point of the struggle is to be ready for the European revolution that will break out in a matter of months. The problem of power should not be posed as one of monarchy vs republic (although of course you can't share power with the monarchy), but rather in terms of whether joining the government offers a way of leading the country with a firm hand in the European crisis accompanying the fall of Germany. This is the compass that we have to follow — not simply the institutional question. In other words, it is possible that even in a republic it might be advisable that the left not be in the government. Power under an English occupation would necessarily mean following an English policy line, and taking weak or strong positions in decisive moments exactly to the extent that this suited the English. Remember, the only card in a losing country's hand is the insurrection card, and we have to get ourselves ready to play it. Naturally we don't say these things to the newspapers, but this is the political line I think we should follow.

Are we up to doing what we propose? I can't guarantee it, because we don't have much in the way of forces available to us. But now with Giunio's help, I hope that for a federalist action we can bring in the federalists of the AP, who are swamped with work for their party. I can only promise you that I will give it every bit of my good will.

Warmest regards.

Angelo[16]

---

[16]Eugenio.

N. 8   30 Novembre 1943

ℰ𝒜𝓋𝒶𝓃𝓉𝒾!

GIORNALE DEL PARTITO SOCIALISTA ITALIANO DI UNITA' PROLETARIA

ITALY WITHOUT A GOVERNMENT

Marshal Badoglio's attempt at Bari to put together a government that represents popular anti-fascist movements and the national will to fight back against the foreign and domestic enemy has failed.

This confirms that it is not behind a monarchy that has nursed the Fascist viper in its bosom for twenty years, nor behind military chiefs tainted by Fascism that the nation can unite to reclaim its destiny and find the courage to face the harsh struggles that await it.

Count Sforza and Benedetto Croce were perfectly right to reject the invitation to collaborate with Badoglio or to form a new government. Count Sforza, who has carried the banner of Italian liberty for twenty years with unmatched pride, was not about to sell out for this king of 28 October 1922 and 10 June 1940. Nor could the Neapolitan philosopher, despite the conservative background of his liberalism, close out his honored life in the role of minister to the Fascist king.

The country demands better. In accordance with the vote of the National Liberation Committee, it calls for a healthy public government, which assumes all the constitutional powers of the state and draws from the investiture of the people the authority and strength to wage a war of liberation alongside the United Nations and to prepare for free debate on the institutional form of the state. [. . .]

Outcasts for twenty years in prison, confinement and exile, we have suffered most from the cynicism of the leaders and many of the intellectual cadres, which we could feel corroding the soul of the nation. What wounded us was the permanent carnival of piazza Venezia, the theater of vice masquerading as virtue, the preening cowardice, the thievery in Spartan or Franciscan disguise, the emptiness posing as enthusiasm.

All this could only end in disaster. And now that the disaster has struck the country, more terrible than in the grimmest forecast, we are left dumbstruck at the irresponsibility of the many people who think only of their own immediate interests, large and small, and take refuge in the decadent dream of Rome as the papal curia, or of the war passing them by and sparing them their small comforts.

Fortunately there is another Italy, an Italy of men who for twenty years have not bent, of workers who can see beyond immediate gain, of young people who have discovered the road to salvation through desolate contemplation of the Fascist carnivals. The possibility of a rebirth of the nation is entrusted to the honest courage of this other Italy, to the power of suggestion that flows from it, to its spirit of sacrifice. [. . .]

N. 9   15 Dicembre 1943

Avanti!

GIORNALE DEL PARTITO SOCIALISTA ITALIANO DI UNITA' PROLETARIA

A SINGLE WATCHWORD

To our comrades all over Italy who want to make themselves useful in the cause of the Italian people we offer a single watchword: fight. To the hesitant, the timid and the uncertain who cannot find their way on their own, to those who would like to resolve all Italy's problems immediately, in hypothetical and arbitrary terms, we single out one inescapable task: destroy Fascism and Nazism. To those who express fears and reservations about the future, we respond that the future is precisely in what we put into this fight, in the ability — which we will have to demonstrate — to eliminate from people, things and institutions the very seed of fascist tyranny. To those who ask us to act, we offer this single principle: respond to oppression with resistance, to retaliation with sabotage, to provocation with armed attack.

N. 10   30 Dicembre 1943

Avanti!

GIORNALE DEL PARTITO SOCIALISTA ITALIANO DI UNITA' PROLETARIA

FOR THE BANDS OF FREEDOM VOLUNTEERS

There are two problems before us, and the fate of the national struggle for liberty depends on solving them. The first is the problem of the government, and we have expressed our views on this on a number of occasions. If the gentlemen in Bari do not understand that their obstinate determination to retain a semblance of power is an obstacle to the rebirth of an Italian fighting force capable of liberating the country, it means their sense of responsibility is deserting them. If this is the case, then the will of the people must in one way or another show them the way out.

The second problem concerns the bands, and it is linked in more than one way to the first one.

The bands arose by spontaneous germination in the aftermath of the September capitulation. A variety of elements have contributed to their composition: soldiers who did not resign themselves to surrender when the royal army suddenly collapsed, young people who went into hiding to escape German or Fascist conscription, anti-Fascists who decided on armed resistance against the Fascist squads that re-assembled under the protection of the Germans, prisoners of war who had escaped from the concentration camps. At first the bands were enormous, but time, supply problems, winter and now and again the fighting thinned them out and in a certain way purged them. Passive elements seeking refuge rather than the fight got tired. Selection favored the strongest and best, and especially those who were aware of the national and political terms of the ongoing struggle. These held out. The others dispersed like dead leaves before the first chill winds of autumn. At the present moment the bands present the dual character of groups of partisans in hiding, and of teams of volunteers who meet whenever the need for defensive or offensive action arises. In the one case and in the other they represent the armed vanguard of the people.

N. 11   12 Gennaio 1943

Avanti!

GIORNALE DEL PARTITO SOCIALISTA ITALIANO DI UNITA' PROLETARIA

A NEW YEAR'S APPEAL TO YOUNG PEOPLE

[. . .] The forces fighting for our rebirth are among the survivors and compatriots of the youth that Mussolini sent to fight in Africa, Greece, and Russia.

The Socialist Party comes to these young people and tells them: You have been deceived and betrayed and you question whether life still has any role and meaning for you. The charades of the "imperial" years have left you bitter. All around you nothing remains but the slimy stench. All that's left of the heroic myths they wasted your time with are the stories of Bibbi's love affair with Claretta, the German drivel of Farinacci, and the robberies of the Pollastrini gangs. The monarchy hiding out with the English doesn't interest you, and you are disgusted with the Mussolini republic that has sprung up in Hitler's camp. Along with the pity that grips your heart for the fate of the country you have a dark feeling of pity for yourself and your lost illusions. You ask yourselves — What to do? But there is no answer.

This answer is what the Socialist Party can give you.

Young workers, young farmers, young technicians, join the freedom volunteers fighting the foreign and domestic enemy, join the organizations of the working class and get ready for the decisive battle for power and for socialism.

Young intellectuals, come back to the rationalist and socialist humanism that will free you from spiritualist gibberish and demiurgic ravings, from Sorel's myth of the sublime and the Nietzschian superman, and will bring you back to reason, science and progress.

Eugenio Colorni: Preface to the "Ventotene Manifesto"[1]

[22 January 1944]

The present writings were conceived and drafted on the island of Ventotene in the years 1941 and 1942. In that unusual environment, under conditions of the most rigid discipline and the despondency of enforced inertia combined with eagerness for imminent liberation, and based on fragmented information painstakingly pieced together, some of us began to re-think the issues that had motivated the actions and positions we had taken in the struggle.

The isolation from concrete political activity allowed for a more detached view and suggested a review of traditional positions and a search for the reasons for past failures, looking not so much at technical errors of parliamentary or revolutionary tactics or at a generically "immature" situation, but rather at deficiencies in the general approach and the fact of having pursued the struggle along the usual fault lines, paying too little attention to what was new and was altering the situation.

In preparation for efficiently fighting the great looming battle for the near future, we felt a need not simply to correct the errors of the past, but to reformulate the terms of the political issues with minds unencumbered by doctrinaire preconceptions or party myths.

Thus it was that in the minds of some of us, the key idea took shape that the basic contradiction responsible for the crises, wars, misery and exploitation afflicting our society was the existence of sovereign states, geographically, economically and militarily distinct, that view other states as competitors and potential enemies, and live in a perpetual state of *bellum omnium contra omnes* with respect to each other.

There are many reasons why this idea, although not new in it-

---

[1]This text is certainly attributable to the pen of Eugenio Colorni. It was published in a volume edited by Colorni himself that appeared in January 1944 under the title *Problemi della federazione europea*, which contained, along with the *Manifesto*, two other documents drawn up by Altiero Spinelli [note by Leo Solari]

self, took on a new significance on the occasion and under the conditions in which it was conceived:

1) First of all, the internationalist solution, which appears on the agendas of all progressive political parties, is in a certain sense considered by each of them to be a necessary and almost automatic consequence of achieving the ends that each of these parties proposes. The democrats maintain that the establishment within each country of the regime they advocate will surely lead to the formation of that unitary consciousness which, passing beyond all cultural and moral frontiers, will constitute the basis, for them indispensable, of a free union of peoples, even in the areas of politics and economics. And the socialists, for their part, think that the establishment of the dictatorship of the proletariat in the various states will in itself lead to an international collectivist state.

Now, an analysis of the modern concept of the state and the interests and feelings linked to it clearly shows that although similarities in internal regimes can facilitate friendly relations and collaboration between one state and another, it is by no means certain that this will automatically or even progressively lead to unification, as long as there are collective interests and feelings associated with maintaining a unity confined within borders. We know from experience that chauvinistic feelings and protectionist interests can easily lead to clash and competition even between two democracies; there is nothing to say that a rich socialist state would necessarily pool its own resources with another much poorer socialist state merely because it was governed by a similar regime.

The abolition of political and economic borders between states, therefore, does not necessarily derive from the simultaneous establishment of a given internal regime in each state; it is an issue in its own right, and must be tackled using appropriate means tailored specifically to it. It is true that it is not possible to be socialists without also being internationalists; but this is due to an ideological connection rather than political and economic necessity, and a socialist victory in individual states does not necessarily lead to an international state.

2) What also urged us to give autonomous prominence to the federalist proposal was the fact that existing political parties, tied to a history of struggles fought within the confines of each nation, are by habit and tradition accustomed to defining all problems on the tacit assumption of the existence of the nation-state and therefore considering problems at the international level to be issues of 'foreign policy' to be resolved through diplomacy and agreements between various governments. This point of view is partly the cause and partly the consequence of the attitude mentioned above whereby, once power has been seized in one's own country, agreement and union with similar regimes in other countries will automatically come about without the need for a political struggle expressly dedicated to this end.

The authors of the present writings, on the other hand, held the deep-rooted conviction that anyone who wishes to pose the problem of the international order as central to the current historical era and treat its solution as a necessary prerequisite to solving all our society's institutional, economic and social problems, must extend this point of view to all issues concerning internal political conflicts and to the attitude of each party as well, even when it comes to the tactics and strategies of the daily struggle. All issues, from constitutional liberty to class struggle, from planning to gaining power and using it, take on a new light when articulated starting from the premise that the primary goal is a united international system. Even political maneuvering — aligning oneself with one or another of the forces at play, highlighting one political catchphrase or another — takes on a very different significance depending on whether the essential aim is to seize power and implement certain reforms within the ambit of each single state, or to create the economic, political and moral prerequisites for the establishment of a federal order that embraces the entire continent.

3) Yet another reason — perhaps the most important — is that while the ideal of a European federation, the precursor to a global federation, may still have seemed a distant utopia a few years ago, it now appears, at the end of this war, to be an achievable goal and

almost within reach. The complete reshuffling of populations that the conflict has provoked in all the countries under German occupation; the need to reconstruct an almost completely wrecked economy on new foundations and to refocus attention on all the problems concerning political boundaries, customs barriers, ethnic minorities, etc.; the very character of this war, in which the national element has so often been overshadowed by the ideological element, with small and medium-sized states surrendering much of their sovereignty to stronger states, and the Fascists themselves replacing the concept of 'national independence' with that of 'living space' — all these elements should be recognized as evidence that the federal ordering of Europe is more topical than ever before.

Forces from all social classes, for reasons that are both economic and idealistic, should be interested in this. It can be approached by means of diplomatic negotiation and popular agitation, and by promoting the study of problems related to the issue among the educated classes, provoking de facto revolutionary conditions from which it will be impossible to turn back. We can do this by influencing the upper echelons of the victorious states and spreading the word in defeated states that only in a free and united Europe will they be able to find salvation and avoid the disastrous consequences of defeat.

It is for this precise purpose that our Movement arose. It is the preeminence, the priority of this problem over all the others afflicting us in the period we are now entering, and the sure knowledge that if we let the situation re-solidify in the old nationalistic molds, the opportunity will be lost forever and our continent will have no lasting peace and well being. All of this is what motivated us to create an autonomous organization whose purpose is to champion the idea of the European Federation as an achievable goal in the post-war period.

We do not hide the difficulties of this, nor the power of the forces ranged on the other side; but it is the first time, we believe, that this problem has been placed on the table of the political struggle not as a distant ideal, but as a pressing, tragic necessity.

Our Movement has for approximately two years now lived a difficult clandestine life under Fascist and Nazi oppression. Its adherents come from the militant ranks of anti-Fascism and are all in the front line of the armed struggle for freedom. We have paid a heavy price in prison for the common cause; our Movement is not and does not want to be a political party. Its character has become increasingly clear: the Movement aims to work with and within the various political parties, not only to bring the internationalist issue to the foreground, but also — most importantly — to ensure that all related political problems are framed from this new perspective, up to now so unfamiliar to the parties.

We are not a political party because, while we actively promote all types of research on the institutional, economic and social structure of the European Federation and take an active part in the struggle to bring it into being, always seeking to identify forces that might act in its favor in the future political situation, we do not want to take an official position on the institutional details — the level of economic collectivization, the degree of administrative decentralization, etc., etc. — that will characterize this future federal body. Suffice it to say that within our Movement these problems are widely and freely discussed and that every political tendency, from communist to liberal, is represented among us. Indeed, almost all our adherents carry weight in one or another of the progressive political parties and all agree in supporting the basic principles of a free European Federation not based on any kind of hegemony or totalitarian order, but endowed with a structural solidity that keeps it from turning into a mere League of Nations.

These principles may be summarized as follows: a single federal army, a single currency, abolition of customs barriers and emigration limits among the Federation's member states, direct representation of citizens in federal assemblies, and a unified foreign policy.

In its two years of life our Movement has spread widely among anti-Fascist groups and political parties. Some of them have publicly expressed their adherence and their sympathy. Others have called on us to collaborate on their policy statements. It would perhaps not be presumptuous to say that it is partly to our credit that the problems of the European Federation are so often discussed in the Italian underground press. Our journal, *L'Unità Europea,* closely follows domestic and international events, taking positions on them with absolute independence.

The present writings, the result of the development of the ideas that led to the birth of our Movement, represent nothing more than the opinion of the authors and do not in any way constitute the position of the Movement itself. They are intended only as a proposal of topics for discussion for anyone who wants to rethink the problems of international political life in the light of the most recent ideological and political experiences, the most up-to-date findings of economics, and the most sensible and reasonable prospects for the future.

They will be followed presently by other studies. Our hope is that they will stimulate an outpouring of ideas, and that in the present atmosphere, alive with the urgent need for action, they will provide the clarity that will make such action ever more resolute, clear-eyed and responsible.

The Italian Movement
for a European Federation

Rome, 22 January 1944

Avanti!

GIORNALE DEL PARTITO SOCIALISTA ITALIANO DI UNITA' PROLETARIA

THE BATTLE FOR ROME WILL BE WON BY THE PEOPLE OF ROME

Rome's Hour

The great battle that has shaken the earth for four years now descends on the walls of Rome. In this deadly struggle, pitting the ancient armies of reaction in horrific Nazi armor against the forces of freedom under the implacable industrial armories of Russia, England and America, victory already crowns the soldier of liberty with a glorious halo.

The booming guns of Moscow celebrating the great victory at Leningrad are answered by the guns of Nettuno announcing the Anglo-Saxon Allies as they approach Italy's capital.

For the people of Rome, the rumble of Allied artillery is not only the proclamation of their coming liberation, but first and foremost a call to arms in the relentless struggle against Hitler's invaders and their infamous Fascist accomplices. For four months the people of Rome have endured the shameful presence of barbarian troops. For four months their hatred and contempt has grown as they have witnessed their own vile betrayal by degenerate Italians. For four months they have gathered weapons in preparation for the avenging clash. Now they thirst for the hour, the great hour, when the clock of history will strike. [. . .]

Their watchword is the fight without quarter against this Nazi enemy that has invaded and ravaged our country, murdered our patriots, and plundered our assets. It is the unrelenting fight against the loathsome Fascist traitors who follow the master Hitler like vile hyenas and have consecrated betrayal, spying and crime as the sinister elemental covenant of their putrefied Fascist "republic."

Fight without quarter, we say, because if a free nation, reborn like our own from widespread devastation, is to avoid dragging along with it the germs of its past corruption, it must, in the powerful words of the great Catholic and socialist Peguy in reference to the Third Republic, not be born in a state of mortal sin.

And to leave unpunished the most monstrous crime ever committed by traitors against their homeland would indeed mean being reborn in a state of mortal sin; it would be a mortal sin not to make the Hitler's bandits pay dearly for their savage violence.

But there is another mortal sin, and it weighs like a curse on our people — the monarchy, oozing treason. The vile and cowardly monarchy, which with its clumsy presence insists on impeding the march of the Italian people towards struggle and victory.

The Roman people know that this obstacle must be removed, and remove it they will. And they will not do it to settle an institutional question that will inevitably be solved by a free constituent assembly on the soil of a liberated homeland: they will do it so that they can move into combat with greater agility.

In accordance with the resolutions of the National Liberation Committee the people of Rome embrace the conviction that the war against the Nazi invader and his Fascist accomplice cannot be waged by the same king and generals who pushed them into a fratricidal conflict against free peoples.

Romans will therefore heed the fighting words from the single body that groups all the anti-Fascist parties in a fraternal union of common intentions, the body that expresses the sovereign will of the Italian people — the National Liberation Committee.

Our weapons are ready, our hearts are prepared, Rome's hour is at hand, and the world will hear the signal for the avalanche of iron and fire that will come down like a whirlwind on the savage invaders and the traitors to the homeland.

EUGENIO COLORNI TO ALTIERO SPINELLI AND ERNESTO ROSSI[1]

[13 February 1944]

Dear Altiero and Ernesto,

I'm writing just to give you a report on recent events because I don't feel much like writing tonight. Since the day of the landings, the work of the teams has of course intensified. On the one hand we use assault teams, and on the other we're preparing a mass action for the first crucial days and for the interregnum period between the Germans and the English. The National Liberation Committee has a very tepid attitude toward the monarchy; they propose to form a provisional municipality in the interregnum period, but they lack the courage to form a temporary government. And in Bari, as you know, they didn't dare demand anything beyond the abdication of the king, meaning implicitly that they would be ready to join a government with Umberto. All the young people in all three parties on the left (PdA, PS, and PC) are unhappy with bland and accommodating politics of this kind, and they let it be known quite clearly. It is likely that the parties will end up coming into a government with the monarchy, and if this happens I think the young people will all break away and form a large new opposition party. And many of them also belong to parties that are outside the CLN (dissident Communists, Republicans, Social-Christians, etc.) and are entirely opposed to a backroom deal with the monarchy. In the PS this disagreement has broken out more violently than in the other parties. The young people (here in Rome a group notable for their intelligence and education) have formed a political committee and have fought openly against the party leadership. There have been dramatic moments when we came within a hair of expulsions, but now things seem to have been smoothed over. The day before yesterday the leadership approved an order of business in which they openly repudiated the

---

[1]Short report published in Paolini, E. (1996) *Altiero Spinelli. Dalla lotta antifascista alla battaglia per lo Federazione Europea. 1920–1948: documenti e testimonianze* (Bologna: Il Mulino) p. 357–58.

Bari policy. This really got on the nerves of the CP and the PdA, who are seen to be in a sense losing the initiative.

Giunio[2] and Giovanni[3] and I have been very active in this group, but within the group we advocate staying in the party for now, and not giving up on the work of the teams. In fact, we are now on the very high-risk team commanded by Giunio. I have been assigned an editorial post with *Avanti!*, and it is not unlikely that in the next reshuffle they'll put me on the executive board. Throughout this uproar we have continued to argue that the problem of the CLN. and the monarchy is nothing but a pretext, and that the real, deeper disagreement is over whether the party should take on the task of simply muddling along administering the country in the difficult years that follow the war, or whether it should instead move in a revolutionary direction in the European crisis that will break out when Germany collapses. Naturally the federalist issue has been constantly at the forefront of this debate. Working with this group we started a party school, which operated with great success. There were five courses: general principles of socialism, general theory of the state, political economy and Marxism, ideologies and political parties, and critical analysis of various revolutions. We will go on with this school as soon as the British arrive, preparing handouts for the courses, and I will be entrusted with organizing the popular university. None of the young people in our group are orthodox Marxists, and they are thus quite open to a revision of the principles of socialism in the direction that you propose. I have the impression, however, that the situation of the PS outside Rome, and especially in Turin and Milan, is much worse than here, indeed all but a failure.

We have published your writings in a very elegant booklet that will be out within three or four days, and I enclose a draft of the frontispiece. I had to write the preface myself because we couldn't get a copy of the Manifesto that you published in Milan. We will sell the first 500 numbered copies at 100 lire each to sponsors, even before the English arrive, and after their arrival the other 2500 copies will go on the market at 30 lire each. We are expecting a great

---

[2]Cerilo Spinelli.
[3]Not identified.

success. The authors will get 15% of the sales of the 2500 non-numbered copies; we figure they will give the movement the numbered copies as a gift. The cost of the printing was 27,000 lire. We are now nearing completion of a facility that will enable us to print our own and other newspapers. (The plant belongs exclusively to the European Federalist Movement). For our paper we have all the material ready, but I don't think it's too important that we bring it out now in this clandestine period teeming with pamphlets, since it would look like just one among many and we would have serious problems with distribution. Especially since your book will be much more effective propaganda. I think instead that we ought to get ready to bring something out every two weeks in the form of a Fascist Critique, as soon as the British get here, but I do not know if we'll manage this because our forces are few and money is scarce.

The collaboration between Giunio, Giovanni and me is working better than we could have imagined. We are very close, and we complement each other. Send news. We've read a letter from Pantagruel[4] and Pessimista[5] and one from Pietro's[6] brother-in-law; that's all we know about you. I also send greetings from Giunio, who is out of Rome on a mission.

Aldo

---

[4]Altiero Spinelli.
[5]Mario Alberto Rollier.
[6]Pietro Nenni.

N. 13   14 Febbraio 1944

Avanti!

GIORNALE DEL PARTITO SOCIALISTA ITALIANO DI UNITA' PROLETARIA

ON THE FRONT LINE

The day when the whole population of Rome is called upon to show their indomitable desire for freedom and rebirth is now close. When the hour strikes for Rome, it must find all of us on the front line, determined to fight in any way we can against Hitler's barbarian hordes and the miserable rabble of so-called republican Fascists who have sold out to Germany. The daily action of the vanguard spearheading the fight, already intensified following the Anglo-American landing at Nettuno, will at a moment's notice spread in a lightning mass uprising that brings us out of the long clandestine phase and explodes into a great battle, with the people as its only true protagonist.

The appeal to citizens for insurrection and open struggle launched in the last few days by the anti-Fascist parties is not dictated by vague sentimental or — even worse — rhetorical motives, but by a clear and precise awareness of the pressing need for the complete and resolute PRESENCE of Rome in the war of liberation which for five months, in parallel with the armies of the United Nations, Italian patriots have been fighting in the Alps and the Apennines, in the countryside and the cities, with arms and propaganda, renouncing the enticements of a comfortable life, the usual habits of work and the natural appeal of family affections, and often making the supreme sacrifice in their irrepressible passion for freedom. It would be too bad for our country if things weren't like this — if freedom, instead of being painfully won by Italians, had to be presented to us as a gift from the outside; and too bad for Rome, the capital, if it were absent at the moment of the decisive test. The fact is, it is in Rome that the still unresolved problems of government and the conduct of the war will in the end need to be tackled; and the moral and physical weight that Roman workers and the citizenry bring to the solution will surely be very great if they are able to follow the glorious example of Naples, and to participate actively and with discipline in the expulsion of the Germans and Fascists. After all the cloying pseudo-Roman rhetoric, the time has finally come for Rome to show its true face. Meanwhile, the danger is the Germans, who in their incurable obtuseness delude themselves that they can avert the inevitable by increasing, hour by hour, the cruelty of their already intolerable oppression. In recent days they have unleashed a brutal wave of violence and terrorism in Rome — mass shootings of political prisoners, arrests and searches everywhere (even in extra-territorial Vatican locations), the appalling torture of people arrested and sometimes their families, roundups of men and women in the city streets. But it is all for nothing. The proliferation of these vicious acts by the Nazi occupiers, with the close collaboration of the republican Fascists and some well-identified functionaries and agents of various police forces, does nothing but increase the hatred Romans feel and harden their determination to fight to free the city and save it from the systematic destruction long planned by the Germans and to avenge the heroic victims of Nazi-Fascist reaction.

No one can hope to escape tomorrow's terrible reckoning — everyone will inexorably face public justice for whatever part they have played, be it large or small, active or passive, by word or deed, in German domination. The warning counts as much for republican Fascists as for officials, and generally for all those who, by supporting the Nazis, have failed in their most elementary duties as Italians. It also applies to the miserable hired pen-pushers for the newspapers who have had the impudence to justify, encourage, and even exalt the crimes the Nazis have perpetrated. No one can hope to save themselves by invoking the pretext of nonexistent official obligations — nonexistent because the so-called Fascist social republic is simply a criminal association paid for by the enemy, not a legal government — or specific selfish personal or family needs, which today must in any case absolutely give way to the higher duty of human and national solidarity in the struggle against the oppressor.

Avanti!

GIORNALE DEL PARTITO SOCIALISTA ITALIANO DI UNITA' PROLETARIA

ALL POWER TO THE NATIONAL LIBERATION COMMITTEES!

The agenda of our party's leadership regarding the resolutions of the Bari Congress has been a great success. It has shown our clear desire to set a moral standard for the country's political life by being perfectly straightforward and saying without the slightest trace of ambiguity what we want and what we don't want, what we can do to maintain and strengthen Italian unity and what we cannot do.

After the Risorgimento democratic parties were in the habit of invoking the theoretical threat of a republic as argumentative blackmail against the monarchy — the expression comes from the author of the *Mulino del Po* — and tolerating the monarchy de facto as an expedient and with mental reservations. This little game has had its day. Twenty years of Fascist dictatorship and the utter ruin of the country in the war that Fascism and the monarchy committed us to against the people's will have put the institutional question on the table not as a theoretical problem, but as an actual life and death necessity for the nation. In the strong words of the Milan edition of our *Avanti!*, "you don't build a new house on a dung heap."

At the same time we cannot resolve Italy's institutional problem under the protection, tutelage or threat of foreign bayonets, even if they are friendly. Leave Hitler and Himmler's republic to the miserable Mussolini. The republic we want is the expression of the will of our people, and this will cannot be expressed before the country is liberated.

Hence the honest and loyal compromise we signed along with all the other anti-fascist parties in the agenda of last October 16th which asserts all the constitutional powers of the state for the special anti-Fascist government, provisionally setting aside both the republic and the monarchy until the meeting of the sovereign Constituent Assembly.

But take care — you say. Won't you risk sacrificing the country's interests to your political feelings and overlooking the problem of the unified struggle against the German invader and his internal accomplices?

But this warning should not be directed at us. Because it is not we who are obstructing the war of liberation, it is Victor Emanuel.

After 1859, when the Piedmont monarchy seemed to be a force that might favor the unity of the nation, Garibaldi did not hesitate to raise the "Italy and Victor Emanuel" flag and even Mazzini sacrificed his republican feelings to his desire for unity. Today the situation is reversed. The monarchy represents an obstacle to the war of liberation and the rebirth of the country — and in spite of this the king clings to his throne.

[. . .] So who will have the responsibility of command?

Who will be in power?

Not the king, who fled Rome on 9 September and left the army to its own devices, not the government that took refuge in Pescara without leaving orders for the resistance, and not Badoglio, who forgot he was chief of the Italian armed forces so he could be chamberlain to Signor Savoy. So not the monarchy.

The seat of power would be empty if the National Liberation Committee didn't occupy it for the purpose of leading the Italian people against the German invader and his Fascist accomplices in conditions such that the Committee appears free of any suspicion of collusion or compromise with the monarchical institution.

Our slogan must therefore be one and one alone: "All power to the National Liberation Committees to wage the war of national liberation until the country can be consulted."

N. 15   16 Marzo 1944

Avanti!

GIORNALE DEL PARTITO SOCIALISTA ITALIANO DI UNITA' PROLETARIA

THE WORKING CLASS ON THE FRONTLINE IN THE STRUGGLE FOR INDEPENDENCE AND FREEDOM

Churchill's Speech

[. . .] On the political side Churchill dedicates a good part of his speech to the Italian situation. Substantially, he said three things. In the first place, Churchill recalls that the armistice was stipulated between the Allied powers and the royal government under Badoglio, which fulfilled the commitments it made. Here it is clear that Churchill is referring particularly to the exemplary behavior of the Italian navy, which deployed its hundred warships against the common enemy.

Secondly, the British prime minister states that he is in doubt as to whether a government representing anti-Fascism would at present have greater authority over the country's armed forces than the monarchic government of Badoglio. Thirdly, after having declared that once Rome is taken there will be a re-examination of the political situation, which in the mind of the British prime minister ought to result in an expansion of the base of the present government to include anti-Fascist forces, he expresses his apprehension that it may be wishful thinking to imagine that a truly democratic government can affirm itself in the eyes of the country while continuing to assert its total autonomy with respect to the Allied governments.

This apprehension on the part of the British prime minister is the key to interpreting the real meaning of his approach to the Italian problem. The Allied governments — allies for us even though we are not yet allies for them — find themselves in a relationship of simple co-belligerence with the royal government of Badoglio. This co-belligerent relationship entails the maximal compliance of Badoglio's monarchical system with the war directives of the Allies. But is this what the Allies want? Is it really in their interests to want this? Or would they instead prefer the total mobilization of all our country's forces against the common enemy? And how then can it not be clear that this total mobilization will benefit decisively from the transformation of co-belligerence into true alliance, which cannot help but have as its legitimate counterpart the total autonomy of the Italian government, even within the frame of the military needs imposed by a common struggle? And what government can the belligerent nations join in a true alliance if not a government that legitimately expresses the will of our country — a government that can lead the fight against the Nazis and their

Fascist accomplices with maximum effectiveness?

[...] We come to the other points in the prime minister's speech, summed up in two postulates concerning legitimacy and efficiency.

With regard to legitimacy, the problem is to decide which government is more legitimate — one representing the forces that have struggled for a quarter century against the same enemy that the whole world is now fighting, or one that up until yesterday was the ally and accomplice of that enemy. The question is answered simply by asking it.

The war now tearing the world apart is nothing more than the epilogue to a long story in which Italian anti-Fascism has been the ignored Cassandra in an opaque and hostile world. It is nothing more than the furious flare-up of an all-consuming conflagration whose first sparks Italian anti-Fascism —

alone, misunderstood, and burning its fingers — tried for twenty years to put out, sparks that many of our present mentors fanned at the time, seeing that the flames that consumed the Peoples' Houses were so beautiful. . . .

We can talk of legitimacy as well, but let us recognize that the historical legitimacy of a government is measured not by the antiquity of its coats of arms, but by its degree of adherence to the most basic causes underlying people's lives and struggles, and to the one true tradition of fidelity to those ideas in whose name the people are called upon to shed their blood.

We are left with the question of efficiency. Concerning which, in our case, the British prime minister has displayed his lack of comprehension!

Eugenio Colorni: Administration or Revolution[1]

[16 March 1944]

The struggle against Nazi oppression and emphatic anti-monarchy partiality are what today unite the main anti-Fascist parties in a brotherhood of intentions that tends to erase their differences in the face of the great work that must be carried out together. And at the same time the need for a total reorganization of the economic base that modern society rests on has become so obvious to all the parties that their programs have increasingly converged. On the theme of economic and social reform, the less there is to preserve and the more to rebuild, the easier it is to reach an agreement; and the war is responsible for pushing us to take giant steps in this direction every day.

It therefore often happens that we meet young people, new to politics, who judge the parties only on the basis of their declared intentions and wonder what the essential differences are among the various programs and whether it might be possible to unify them. They have a tendency (perhaps prompted by memories of Fascist propaganda) to see all divisions as non-essential and based on cliquish or personal interests. They feel an overwhelming need to see the political arena reorganized into a limited number of neatly defined currents able to offer the people simple and comprehensive phrases that clearly express their needs.

These young people are not completely wrong. Too many of the motives presently dividing the anti-Fascist parties come from old disagreements perpetuated more by tradition than by any real idealist necessity. There are too many doubles on today's Italian political chessboard: Liberals and Labor Democrats, Republicans and Action Party, Social-Christians and Catholic Communists, Socialists and Communists and Dissident Communists. As you can see, we do not exclude ourselves from the list, and for quite some time we have

---

[1]This article was published in the Rome edition of the clandestine *Avanti!*, n. 15. Re-published in Solari, L., *Eugenio Colorni. Ieri e sempre* (Venezia: Marsili, 1980) p. 157–62, and in Colorni, E. (2019), part III, chap. 4.

expressed our firm desire to get beyond the difficulties, misunderstandings and suspicion that stand in the way of forming a single
great proletarian party.

But although many artificial divisions can be eliminated, there
are others that will necessarily remain, because they have to do
with the ideological and social structure of our society. Conservative and progressive trends exist and will continue to exist among
the anti-Fascist parties — and the public should learn to recognize
them even apart from the programs the parties formulate.

Is there presently a criterion that allows us to distinguish a conservative from a progressive party in the light of the actual positions they take in current politics? We believe there is — and that it
is to be sought in the way they put forward the problem of power.
Everyone agrees that real anti-Fascist forces will need to come to
power for the essential purpose of efficiently leading the war of liberation alongside the United Nations. But what will they do with
this power when, in the not so distant future, the war is over and
the great task of reconstruction is at hand?

There are those who believe that the essential purpose of taking
power is to do as little harm as possible while guiding the country out
of the tragic difficulties the fascist war plunged it into; to extinguish
this failed legacy in such a way that people suffer as little as possible;
to administer the state so that it settles gradually into shape; to earn
merit in the eyes of the victorious powers. These are worthwhile tasks,
without doubt, that no responsible party, least of all ours, would back
away from. But this sort of limited vision entails viewing the future
of Europe and the world from a series of perspectives that we do not
hesitate to call reactionary. It entails first of all the view that at the end
of this war everything will remain as before internationally, except
for a few shifting frontiers and modifications in power relations between various countries; it entails believing that nations' sovereignty
and independence will remain intact, except for a few sanctions the
victors will want to impose; it entails interpreting today's frequent-
ly heard references to 'independence' and 'self-determination' in the
most small-minded and archaic way — in the sense, that is, that each
country will go on as a self-contained political, economic and military unit and will look after its own reconstruction — essentially em-

ploying its own internal resources behind the protection of customs barriers and if necessary accepting the support of other powers in the form of diplomacy or financial credit.

Anyone who comes forward to contend for power on the basis of this view cannot help but view the job as one of ordinary — we could even say extraordinary — administration. The purpose is a return to 'normalcy,' which essentially means the status quo ante. Take the country back to where it was before the beginning of the tragic adventure that ended so disastrously; from there, take up the struggle again, maybe with more daring ideas this time, taking care not to fall into the errors of the past.

With a greater or lesser degree of conscious awareness, many view the problem of power in these terms. But they do not comprehend the enormity of the crisis that engulfs us. They do not realize that we are moving into a preeminently revolutionary era at the international level, and that it is only by participating decisively in this great movement that we can hope to make a conclusive contribution to the well-being of our country and the progress of humanity. The crisis that will soon erupt with the collapse of Germany and will surely strike the Balkan countries, probably along with Scandinavia and France, may well take on the aspect of a great European revolution in which the entire political, economic and social orientation of our continent is called into question. All institutional problems will be re-formulated from this perspective; all social reforms will take on a new meaning in this framework. It will not do to object that the winners alone will decide the essentials of Europe's new orientation, and that all that remains for the people on the losing side is to work within the imposed framework. Even now, in all the countries subjected to German occupation, revolutionary movements are in action that will certainly not respond to the problems of reconstruction as passive bystanders; at this moment, even in England and America (not to speak of Russia), progressive forces are in motion, putting forward non-imperialist solutions aimed at eliminating once and for all the danger of repeated warfare through a total renewal of the European economic and social structure on a unified basis.

The purpose of a progressive party aiming to win power in its country is to ready itself and ready the people for this great event; to establish the foundations for the active participation of the entire nation in this total renewal of the very basis of our social coexistence; to be an actor, not a spectator or, worse yet, a blind follower in the decisive events we are about to face.

The fault line today between the various political parties, which the young people vainly look for in contorted program formulations, is this — administration or revolution. We are decidedly for the second alternative.

ᴄ𝒜𝓋𝒶𝓃𝓉𝒾!

GIORNALE DEL PARTITO SOCIALISTA ITALIANO DI UNITA' PROLETARIA

AT THE GRAVE OF THE 500 SHOT IN ROME THE NATION IS WARNED OF THE COMING STRUGGLE!

In the tragic and shifting fortunes of the occupation, in the daily and hourly war going on between the invaders and the people, the massacre of the 500 shot on 24 March is one of the most sorrowful of events, but it is at the same time a warning and an omen.

The warning is for those who have not understood what the values are that are at stake in the present conflict. The omen is in spite of everything an omen of victory, because when the enemy is forced by the infernal logic of his crime to turn to this sort of tactics it means that like a beast besieged in his lair, he can no longer control his reactions.

We dip our flags at this, the grave of our brothers, many of whom were comrades in arms who shared our aspirations. We need not speak words of revenge.

Revenge for us is in our dauntless desire not to let ourselves be beaten down, not to give up the fight whatever the stakes, to go forward even when our hearts are torn by pity for the victims and by horror toward their murderers.

Pity for the fallen, whose memory will be forever honored; pity for the families, who as soon as it is possible will receive the concern that anyone deserves who suffers for the common cause; pity for humanity, reduced by the fascist war to such abominable extremes.

Beyond the graves, forward!

n. 1   1 Maggio 1944

Rivoluzione Socialista

ORGANO DELLA FEDERAZIONE GIOVANILE DEL PARTITO SOCIALISTA DI UNITA' PROLETARIA

The 1st of May: The armed proletariat salutes the dawn of the socialist revolution in Europe

NEITHER QUIRINALE NOR AVENTINO

After Naples our watchword remains unchanged — neither Quirinale nor Aventino.

In the wake of the Bari congress we stated that the anti-Fascist group directing its attacks against Victor Emanuel had become embroiled in the moral issue and had side-stepped the real Italian political problem that required setting aside the monarchy as a necessary condition of the parties of the National Liberation Committee for joining the government. The executive council was born on the inclined plane that led to the royal palace. Bari was the antechamber of Naples. The collaborationist thunderbolts launched by Togliatti when he landed in Naples did nothing but precipitate a solution suspended in the stagnant waters of the south.

Seen from this side of the Garigliano, the solution to the crisis looks like the territorially and temporarily contingent result of a static situation in which the transcendence of the Allied war has ended up overwhelming the importance of the political problem.

The results of Naples mean treating the political and military problems as two autonomous elements only somewhat affecting one another and postponing the first till after the second; in other words, forcing the bisecting of the democracy-war duo — that is, of the one common flag that the forces fighting in the invader's citadel can hoist.

The result of the prolonged stasis in military operations, brutally splitting Italy in two, has been to break apart the Italian political problem. Whereas in free Italy the war conditions the politics, in occupied Italy it is the politics that determines the volunteer war.

Today more than ever, therefore, our slogan really means something; only under this banner will the liberation struggle be able to regain its single political platform and will the wall erected by political and military contingency along the Garigliano collapse as a tactical expedient of the war. If Naples meant something different and the tension between anti-Fascism and monarchy and between democracy and monarchy were not taking on a new political shape, then we would have to admit sadly that the structure of the new democratic forces in Italy had dramatically collapsed. Eight months of tireless effort to present the Italian problem to the country and the world in its only possible terms would have been wiped out. Political chaos would have replaced the natural Italian democratic process.

Reducing the institutional problem to a moral issue against the man or the institution frames the problem in such a way that it falls prey to the easy game of the proponents of the Machiavellian viewpoint that twenty years of "reasons of state" have sown in the political mentality of the masses.

We maintain that the institutional question is not only a core problem for Italian democracy, but that in the present dynamic situation it is the problem of problems for revolutionary socialism.

Historically, institutional agnosticism in the body of socialism was one of the most damaging results of reformist sclerosis. The institution of the monarchy has never been and can never be neutral with respect to the proletariat. At a time when the country, tragically worn out by two terrible wars, is almost tyrannically proletarian, the monarchy becomes our main internal enemy.

For us it is the monarchy in general, as the focus of all the reactionary and conservative forces, that is responsible for the Italian people's past and present calamities. Its continued post-catastrophe existence guides conservative efforts and brings out new reactionary positions. Its monstrous survival falsifies the true plane of Italian politics by determining political alignments that are completely discordant with the real situation; it prevents national consciousness from immediately and smoothly reaching a level which it may otherwise only arrive at later through a new long period of grief and ruin.

Revolutionary action granting full constitutional powers to a special government and setting aside for the time being both the monarchy and the republic means setting the only conditions that would allow the Italian people to express their sovereign will concerning the future form of the state. It means blocking the development at a national level of anti-historical and reactionary positions that would do nothing but fuel a future civil war — even more dangerous insofar as it would allow the intervention of conflicting foreign interests.

The monarchy, skillfully playing the international game and exploiting the weak cohesion among internal democratic forces, has managed to confront the anti-Fascist assembly with the apparently drastic choice of unconditional collaboration with the institution or intransigent absenteeism.

We reject both these alternatives — neither Quirinale nor Aventino.

[. . .]

The Italian people ask for the union of the political forces that must wage their war, but in no way can they accept a government that by its very composition falsifies the war's revolutionary aim. The institutional question is the proving ground for Italian political parties.

Starting today it divides real forces from phantom forces. It separates forces that are carried to power by the people from those who hope for power so they can impose themselves on the people. It divides those who have within themselves the revolution that is in the nature of things from those who feel called by administration and re-normalization. Occupied Italy has raised its unanimous voice in the agendas of the national liberation committees of the north and center of the peninsula — no collaboration with the monarchy!

25 July was certainly a farce, but 8 September was tragedy. On 25 July the palace conspiracy for the exclusive purpose of dynastic rescue automatically brought to the surface the antifascist line-up of twenty years before, but since September 8th the war in the enemy citadel has elucidated new values, created new understandings, and given new meaning to Italian political life. Let us have the courage to say it — there are now two dates and two Italys. The Italy of 8 September has chosen its path, set the goals of its war, and whatever happens now, it will not allow the true terms of the problem of democracy to be falsified or the true meaning of the revolution, which is the only possible meaning of this war, to be misrepresented.

N. 17   6 Maggio 1944

Avanti!

GIORNALE DEL PARTITO SOCIALISTA ITALIANO DI UNITA' PROLETARIA

THE PARTY LEADERSHIP DEFINES THE SOCIALIST POSITION TOWARDS THE NEW BADOGLIO GOVERNMENT AND THE PROBLEMS OF UNIFIED ACTION AND ANTI-FASCIST UNITY

The Directorate of the Socialist Party:

faced with the situation created in southern Italy with the turn of the Communist Party, the vote of the Bari Congress, which saw the establishment of a lieutenancy of the kingdom as a sufficient condition for the participation of the anti-Fascist parties in the government, the decision of the council of the southern Socialist sections to authorize Socialist participation in order to strengthen the war effort and maintain anti-Fascist and proletarian unity, and faced with the consequent formation of a coalition government including both the anti-Fascist parties and the monarchy-Badoglio forces; while recognizing that because of its leadership and the monarchical form of its investiture the new government does not re-

flect the will expressed by the people of occupied Italy over eight months of uninterrupted struggle for freedom, and is not suited to the country's need for democracy; maintains toward it a position of autonomy, which nevertheless entails total adherence to whatever measures are taken to intensify the war against Nazi-Fascism; and charges all socialists and workers to persevere in their will to expel from power the institutions, forces, institutes and men responsible for the twenty-year Mussolinian dictatorship and the Fascist war.

23 April 1944.

N. 17   6 Maggio 1944

cAvanti!

GIORNALE DEL PARTITO SOCIALISTA ITALIANO DI UNITA' PROLETARIA

THE YOUTH FEDERATION OF OUR PARTY AND THE NEWSPAPER "THE SOCIALIST REVOLUTION"

With joy and pride we greet the rebirth of the Youth Federation of the Socialist Party. These young people, born and educated after 1922, who have miraculously passed through two decades of totalitarian Fascist life without letting it contaminate them and who today fight at our side with the ardor of their youth and the cold decisiveness of committed revolutionaries — these young people reaffirm the justice and fecundity of the cause we are fighting for. Their trust and consensus assure us that we are on the right track and encourage us to continue on it. They have shown their maturity by uniting in their own federation — which is not intended simply as an offshoot of the central organs of the party, but a body with a life of its own that will be one of the vital elements in the active exchange of ideas and energy that is an essential feature of our party.

*The first issue of the combat organ of the Youth Federation, entitled So-*cialist Revolution, *has been released. We note with pleasure that the line our party has taken in the recent governmental crisis has been fully shared by the young people, who in this have shown notable maturity of judgment. We encourage everyone to read the new paper, and we wish it a long and fruitful life of facts and ideas.*

Eugenio Colorni: Report for Altiero Spinelli and Ernesto Rossi

[11 May 1944]

Federalist activity: Most of this took the form of an initiative that G.[1] will tell you about and which could have provided us ample breathing space, even from the financial viewpoint. It had been fully launched and had begun to work successfully, when there was a blunder. We still hope that all has not been lost.

The booklet has been remarkably successful and everywhere rated as the best thing to come out in recent times. Its biggest success was in the Action Party and among the Social Christians — among those, that is, who are engaged in building a socialist ideology free of Marxist myths. The liberals also received it favorably, though with some measure of reserve. In the socialist camp, on the other hand, it was greeted with suspicion in leadership circles, like a book by an adversary.

The request for a delegation for the Federalist Congress[2] was accepted only by the Social Christians who delegated Moreno[3] and the Republicans who delegated Cipriano. The socialists have said that they do not fully understand what the movement is; if it is something like "secular patronage" then they tip their hat but do not want to participate; if it is indeed serious, they fear it's a pawn in the British game. I had prepared a proxy letter containing a commitment not to characterize the federation as anti-Russian or even as an extra-Russian bloc; but they did not accept it. Instead, they are going to send Rodolfo[4] as an observer whose task will be to report back. The liberals have done the same, and will send the old master Empirico.[5] I do not know yet

---

[1]G.: Giunio: Cerilo Spinelli. "The second issue of *Socialist Revolution*," recalled Leo Solari (1964, p.41), "like some issues of *Avanti!, Italia Libera, Risorgimento Liberale,* and *Europa Unita,* were printed by a clandestine printing press organized by Eugenio Colorni with the help of the Socialist Youth Federation, a press that was subsequently discovered and invaded by agents of the PAI [Italian African Police] and the Police."
[2]The Assembly of European Liberation Movements, which had already met in March 1944 and had planned additional sessions.
[3]Moreno: Guglielmo Usellini.
[4]Rodolfo Morandi.
[5]Luigi Einaudi.

if it will be possible to send official letters on these assignments; but consider [. . .] my indications as formal invitations.

I was going to bring out a little magazine here. I do not know if we can manage it. In any case, we've already made a commitment to collaborate regularly with a newspaper that will most likely be entitled "Europe" and, while not an organ of the MFE, will have decidedly federalist leanings and will have on board many young members of the PS and the PdA.

The Social Christians have asked to join the movement en masse. We have said they can join one at a time. We are now putting together an expanded leadership committee that will include (as individuals not officially representing parties) a Republican (Breitarme[6]), a PdA member (Ostinato or Pipeta[7]), a Social Christian, and a Liberal, along with the executive committee that has operated up to now, composed of Giunio, Luisa[8] and myself (all three from the PS).

I wanted to send you news of the political situation, but I don't have time due to the incident that occurred. I will do so if, as I foresee, G. doesn't leave tonight.

Regards

E.

11 May 44

---

[6]Giorgio Braccialarghe.

[7]Ostinato has not been identified, Pipeta is Manlio Rossi Doria.

[8]Giunio: Cerilo Spinelli; Luisa: Luisa Villani Usellini.

N. 18   20 Maggio 1944

Avanti!

GIORNALE DEL PARTITO SOCIALISTA ITALIANO DI UNITA' PROLETARIA

ON THE EVE OF THE COMING DECISIVE EVENTS, THE WATCHWORD IS NATIONAL INSURRECTION

ROMANS:
THE IMPENDING MOMENT

We are moving into the decisive phase of the war. The lightning recapture of Sevastopol after a bloody three-day battle indicates that the Soviet army, after the leap that took them in less than a year from the Volga to the Dniester and the Danube, is ready to resume the offensive from the East. In the West, the formidable aerial battles of the Anglo-Americans over Germany, France and Belgium are the prelude to the invasion. Every day between five and eight thousand airplanes hammer Germany, reducing cities to rubble, destroying factories, and disrupting transport. On the Italian front the troops have moved to the offensive.

In this way the military preconditions are falling into place for the popular action which in France as in Belgium, in the Netherlands as in Norway, in Czechoslovakia as in Denmark will be needed in support of the offensive against Hitler's fortress which is about to be unleashed simultaneously from the east, west and south.

The objective of the popular forces in Italy during this phase of the war can be summarized in two compelling and definitive words — national insurrection.

National insurrection against the Nazi invader, national insurrection against the remaining Fascist tools acting as the invader's police, and national insurrection against Fascism's accomplices.

Everyone needs to prepare for this decisive struggle with a fearless heart, with unwavering dedication to the cause, which is everyone's, but also with an awareness of the goal, which must be pursued or achieved by stubborn and patient daily effort.

What this goal is, is stated yet again in the rallying cry of the socialists of Northern Italy. The goal is a Socialist Republic. The socialists know very well that the road to a Socialist Republic cannot be covered in a leap — that there will be stops, detours and backtracking. But they also know that nothing is done until everything is done. And that twenty years of struggle and sacrifice will have been in vain if all the forces of the past are not liquidated forever.

Eugenio Colorni: Revolution from Above?[1]

[20 May 1944]

When we speak of revolution the way things are now, several factors must be kept in mind that make the present situation very different from the one that came about at the end of the last war. At that time, even though they intervened substantially in the internal situation of the defeated nations from an economic, financial and military standpoint, the victorious states essentially left them free to choose the internal regime they preferred. Germany, Austria, Greece, Poland, and Turkey were allowed to carry out their own political development practically undisturbed; only Russia had to defend its revolution against forces supported and armed by the Western powers. The principle of "non intervention" belonged to the political morality of the period between the two wars — and the Fascists were the first to break it, on the occasion of the war in Spain.

Today this principle is absolutely no longer valid. And even though there is still talk of the people's self-determination, by now everyone knows perfectly well that the winning states will not leave the losers to their own devices in the crucial crisis that is about to arrive — indeed, has arrived — in this final stretch of the Second World War. The Fascist experience has alerted everyone to the decisive influence the regime within a state can have on the politics of the whole continent — the winners will closely monitor political developments in the defeated countries so as to block any chauvinistic backsliding that might jeopardize the new equilibrium.

Add to this the now widespread public feeling that the various ideologies are no longer represented by the different parties with their large mass organizations, but rather by the states that have championed of them, in this typically ideological war. For the man in the street, communism means Russia, democracy means America and Britain, fascism Germany, and in the basic consciousness

---

[1]This article was published in the Roman edition of clandestine *Avanti!* n, 18. Republished in Solari, L., *Eugenio Colorni. Ieri e sempre* (Venezia: Marsilio, 1980) p. 163–67. Now in Colorni (2019) p. 11–112.

of the masses, fighting for one or the other of these political forms also means leaning on one or the other of these states. The victors themselves are perfectly aware of this, and often view the parties in the conquered countries as pawns in their international game, favoring and opposing this or that combination, depending on the requirements of their own European and world politics.

So when we talk about revolution today, these elementary facts need to be taken into account.

It may be that we have seen the end of the era of great mass movements crucial to the future life of a people, the romantic era of revolution as a people's rising in which fluctuations in popular favor are decisive for the life of a nation. Today, the scope of the game has widened, and the ties of interdependence between a country's internal regime and the general political framework have multiplied. Every shift in balance even in a peripheral area has repercussions at the center, so that world political leaders can no longer consider the will of the people in any country as an autonomous fact with its own developmental trajectory, but must view it as an element in an extremely complex game in which all the strings must be kept firmly under control.

Must we conclude from all this that if there is a revolution, it will be a revolution from above, brought about or even imposed by the winners? Must we gloomily resign ourselves to no longer having anything to say about our destiny, to being almost pawns in a game whose course we cannot influence? Must we limit our activity to going along with the plans of whichever winning power we are aligned with, taking its every policy maneuver as a directive we simply have to get used to?

We do not believe this for a second. We believe that opposition to this tendency is one of the essential reasons for our party's existence. In assessing the function of mass movements and the free expression of popular will in the present situation, we must consider the fact that these same winning powers have not yet begun to decide what political line they will follow with respect to postwar problems. Their opinions are far from unequivocal, and even in their own minds they have conflicting tendencies that can generally be seen as reactionary and imperialistic, tending to reduce the defeated countries to simple spheres of influence, and as progressive tendencies that aim to radically and definitively resolve all the social, economic, national and state contradictions that have brought us this war and would lead to the perpetuation of the present state of chaos if they were not eliminated with a clean break.

It is into this still uncertain and fluctuating context, in the current delicate political moment, that mass actions must decisively move. Their purpose is to influence public opinion, chancellors' offices, military headquarters: to show what can be done and what cannot be done. A clear "no" from the people and from the parties that represent them can today be decisive in causing the re-evaluation of a situation and radical changes of attitude in the ruling circles of the countries that hold our destiny in their hands.

n. 2   25 Maggio 1944

Rivoluzione Socialista

ORGANO DELLA FEDERAZIONE GIOVANILE DEL PARTITO SOCIALISTA DI UNITA' PROLETARIA

From conspiracy to combat, from the Cell to the Battalion — these are the watchwords of the Socialist Youth as we approach insurrection

REVOLUTION:
On the eve of insurrection

Young fighters of the Roman underground army, pressed sharply without pause for nearly a year by a mighty and merciless enemy served by the most abject rejects of a decaying regime, you have endured even at the cost of unspeakable sacrifices that often saw you put to the ultimate test.

In the country's darkest hour, with all our values at the point of sinking into chaos, you have, with your blood and your hope, once again brought to life an incorporeal, impassable Piave.

The adversary, despite having long raged against the unhappy people of this city, now falters and retreats.

Distraught with the fear of righteous vengeance, the oppressors are preparing to abandon the scene of their misdeeds. The fiery hour of insurrection finally approaches, the hour you have awaited with feverish anxiety, eager to offer final proof of your dedication to the cause.

The comrades slaughtered at Forte Bravetta or in the caves of S. Callisto, and the many led slowly to their deaths in the torture chambers of Via Tasso are waiting for you to prove now that their sacrifice was not in vain.

Comrades, do not betray the Fallen! On the eve of insurrection, your watchwords must be: From conspiracy to combat, from the cell to the battalion, from Rome to the Brenner Pass.

As always on the eve of a decisive battle, look deep inside yourselves for that intimate sense of mission that moves those who in action face the supreme sacrifice every day.

You know that Rome cannot be a mere accident of geography in the path of the war. On the contrary — here, where you have endured the hardest trials, the war must take on its true meaning; it is here that it will throw off its haphazard appearance and emerge as a war of liberation from the world of the past, from old fascisms and old democracies, a war for socialism and true freedom for workers everywhere.

If the old Fascist Monarchy were to set foot in Rome again, it would mean that for Italy and the civilized world the liberation of our capital was no more than a geographical fact.

It is in Rome that Italian history will start over.

EUGENIO COLORNI: TRIBUTE TO LOPRESTI[1]

[19 August 1944]

There are words that we hesitate to apply to Giuseppe Lopresti only because they are too commonly used in the compassionate rhetoric of obituaries. He was truly — and not only today, after his martyrdom — the best, the most serious, the most sensible, the most profoundly pure of our youth. He was 25 years old. He held a degree in law and was in his second year of philosophy; he was intelligent and open to any cultural issue, and with his passionate interest in religious questions as well, it seemed that all roads were open to him.

He approached us with extreme naturalness, as if we were a group he had long been a part of. We felt no hint in him of the distance or detachment that might have come from his having grown up in a fascist climate. Thanks to him we began to appreciate and love this wonderful new generation that now fights alongside us and that seems to have slipped as if by magic through twenty years of fascism without being soiled by it; bringing on the contrary a deeper need to live life consciously and intensely. Beppe brought us close to this youthful world to which we are now so irrevocably bound; this world of which he was in many ways the spokesperson and symbol.

He immediately distinguished himself in our military organization as one of the most reliable and efficient elements. He was entrusted with extremely delicate assignments. Even though he was young and had only been in contact with us for a short time, he was one of our leaders. And he undertook these difficult and risky jobs with utter tranquility, without the slightest presumption, with that modest cheerfulness so common in strong people, people with a clear conscience. For him, the duty to sacrifice himself and to give his own life was something obvious, not even worth talking about. And he showed it under Nazi torture, taking all responsibility on himself.

I saw him only a few minutes before his arrest; he was concerned about a worsening situation, intent on doing whatever was necessary to

---

[1]From *Avanti!* 19 Aug. 1944. Now in Colorni, E., *La scoperta del possibile. Scritti politici*, ed. Luca Meldolesi (Soveria Mannelli: Rubbettino, 2017) p. 205–07.

save what could still be saved. I will never forget his alert and thought-ful face, already holding a premonition of the death that lay in wait.

The Fascists enjoy their inhuman vengeance, but there is one thing they will never know, because they lack the moral standing to understand it, and that is what human values, what spiritual riches they deprive us of with their blind violence. But this, the reason for our terrible pain, is also the source of our fiercest pride.

INDEX OF NAMES

INDEX OF SUBJECTS

www.ingramcontent.com/pod-product-compliance
Lightning Source LLC
Chambersburg PA
CBHW062101080426
42734CB00012B/2715